100 GREATEST CYCLING CLIMBS OF
SPAIN

A GUIDE TO THE FAMOUS CYCLING MOUNTAINS OF MAINLAND SPAIN PLUS **MALLORCA** AND THE **CANARY ISLANDS**

SIMON WARREN

vp

Vertebrate Publishing, Sheffield
www.adventurebooks.com

100 Greatest Cycling Climbs of Spain
A guide to the famous cycling mountains of mainland Spain
plus Mallorca and the Canary Islands
Simon Warren

VP

First published in 2023 by Vertebrate Publishing.

VERTEBRATE PUBLISHING
Omega Court, 352 Cemetery Road, Sheffield S11 8FT, United Kingdom.
www.adventurebooks.com

Front cover: Picón del Fraile.
Photography by Simon Warren unless otherwise credited.

A CIP catalogue record for this book is available from the British Library.

ISBN: 978-1-83981-196-8 (Paperback)
ISBN: 978-1-83981-197-5 (Ebook)

10 9 8 7 6 5 4 3 2 1

Vertebrate Publishing is committed to printing on paper from sustainable sources.

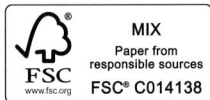

FSC
www.fsc.org

MIX
Paper from
responsible sources
FSC® C014138

Printed and bound in Europe by Latitude Press.

FOR CHAR, LUX AND RYDER

CONTENTS

Riders struggling
on the evil slopes
of La Camperona
(page 93) in 2014.

Vuelta a España

There is no BEST Grand Tour; each is a celebration of its respective country's geography, culture and love for cycling. That said, of the three, the Vuelta a España will always be the third. There's no way to sugar-coat it. Just as the Tour de France will always be number one (sorry, Giro fans), the Vuelta will always prop up the rear, and not simply because of its current place on the calendar. It's just the natural order of things. Regardless of personal preference or popularity, this is the way it goes: France, Italy, then Spain.

First run in 1935, some 32 years after the inaugural Tour de France, its early development was interrupted by various wars, however it's been a continuous annual event since 1955. Like the Tour de France, it is run over three weeks, with mountain stages, time trials and flat stages, but unlike the Tour where the leader is dressed in a yellow jersey, in the Vuelta this hallowed garment is red.

Although now held in late summer, for 60 years it was run in the spring, therefore making it not the last but the first of the big three each year. In a bid to free it from clashing somewhat with the Giro d'Italia, the decision was made in 1995 to move it to its current home in September.

This helped the Vuelta attract a better-quality field, made it the perfect preparation for the World Championships which had moved to October, and also gave those riders who'd had a bad Giro or Tour the opportunity to salvage their season. This has given rise to the saying, 'There's always the Vuelta', as whenever a star crashes in Italy or France, they can recover then head to Spain a few months later to fight for victories hitherto denied them.

The Vuelta is far more than just a 'last chance saloon' for star riders, or a training ground for others though; the Vuelta is very much its own race, especially in my eyes because it's the climber's Grand Tour.

The Vuelta is all about crazy mountaintop finishes, sometimes as many as eight per race, and each year it seems to find more outlandish roads up which to send the peloton. Old goat tracks, concrete service roads, dead ends in the middle of nowhere that finish on a patch of land no larger than a postage stamp. If there is a will, and there is a will, then it seems there will always be a way.

This unquenchable desire to entertain fans and torture riders has brought us many of the delights in this book, from the Angliru all the way to Los Machucos, and much more in between. Each year when the route is announced, it's a case of what on earth have they found this year? What insane roads will they shock us with this time around? And we are rarely disappointed.

As yet, they haven't plucked up the courage to take the race right to the top of Pico Veleta, or to Roque de los Muchachos, but I'm sure it's only a matter of time. Stay tuned.

Approaching the summit
of Pico Veleta. CAN
YOU BELIEVE IT!

Viva España

France? Tick. Italy? Tick. It's about time I did Spain then, I guess!

In the 12 years I've been making these guides, I've never been more excited to release a book. There are so many amazing roads in here, so many classic ascents that will delight, amaze and, at times, outright terrify you. In previous books, I have usually singled out one climb that stands above all others and rewarded it with a Spinal Tap-esque 11/10, but in this book there are THREE! That's right, three roads so off the charts that you simply have to see them to believe them.

This project began way back in the summer of 2014. The ink had only just dried on my guide to France when an opportunity arose to make an impulse visit to chase the Vuelta around Asturias for four days; I jumped at it. Travelling with my good friend Owen Cooper, we flew into northern Spain for a long weekend of brutal roads, blazing sun and lots of flat cider. We would catch three days of race action, but more important than that was a date with the mighty Alto de l'Angliru. Back in the days before I swallowed my pride and fitted a compact chainset to my bike, I turned up, chest puffed out with a lowest gear of 39x28 and absolutely zero fear of what lay ahead. A climb had never stopped me before, I had done everything from Hardknott Pass to the Galibier on that gear, but as I was to find out, to my

eternal shame, the Angliru is a whole different ball game.

About three kilometres from the summit, once I had exhausted the art of zigzagging (riding from one side of the road to the other in an attempt to minimise the impact of the slope), it was either snap my knees or unclick and put a foot down. I was crestfallen. Never before had a mountain road stopped me, but as the clock was ticking and I'd put in plenty of effort already, I ran in my cleats to a point where some sanity returned and I remounted and finished the job. I'd been beaten though, and the reputation of the Angliru was well and truly intact. One day I'd return – this was not over!

The project was then put on hold for over six years as I completed my Italian book, but in the spring of 2019 it was time to get back to it. In the interim period, and after the gargantuan effort of covering all of Italy, I'd decided to make life easy for myself and simply compile a book on the climbs of the Spanish

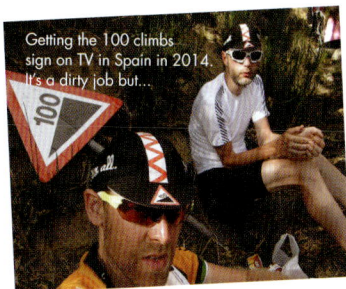

Getting the 100 climbs sign on TV in Spain in 2014. It's a dirty job but...

islands, Mallorca and the Canaries. These were the perennially popular fair-weather venues for us northern Europeans looking for some winter warmth, so I resolved they would be my focus. I soon realised though that I would be selling myself and you the readers short, and as there was so much to discover on the mainland, the book would have to be a more comprehensive volume.

I did, however, start with a trip to Mallorca, family in tow, and couldn't wait to experience its famed roads for the first time. Until then I'd never indulged in a 'training camp' or 'mates cycling holiday'. The last time I'd been to the island was in 1997 with my wife and we spent seven days drinking multicoloured cocktails out of plastic coconuts. This would be, in 47 years, the first time I'd taken a bike there, and wow, right away I could see its attraction. It's neat, compact, the roads are perfect and there are riders everywhere. None of the climbs are hard (unless you make them hard), and if you do take your family, they can relax by the pool while you escape for a couple of hours in the morning before you all head off

Lunch at the summit of Roque de los Muchachos. Mindblowing.

sightseeing in the afternoon. Sorted.

Following Mallorca, it was off on a triple-island raid to Tenerife, La Gomera and La Palma. Four days with Ben Lowe and Paul Morgan on a trip which even by my standards was manic. We had just a few days to visit three different islands and tick off eleven climbs including the mighty Teide on Tenerife and the incomparable Roque de los Muchachos on La Palma. Utilising every minute of available daylight, the schedule was built around the ferry timetables that would get us from island to island as, fuelled by pizza and tortilla, we smashed climb after climb . Highlights were the double ascent of Teide where I was lucky enough to share the road with a young Remco Evenepoel, and our day on Roque de los Muchachos where Ben and I climbed 5,157 metres in just 148 kilometres and got into so much trouble we had to flag down a German camper van and beg them for food so we could make it home.

Later that year, it was time to pack the family and my bike into our old Octavia to tick off everything from Pamplona to Ponferrada via the great cities of Bilbao, Santander and, of course, Donostia (San

Mallorca 1997 where the drinks were blue.

Sebastián). Having never visited this hotbed of gastronomic delights before, we fell in love with it in an instant. The pintos, the wine, the intoxicating atmosphere – as soon as we left, we vowed to return. Also on this trip was my long-overdue return to the Angliru. No climb beats me and gets away with it, so as dawn broke one morning, I set off from Oviedo, this time with a 34 on the front to go with the 28 at the back, determined to regain my reputation. It wasn't easy, but I did it, and once again my CV could read 'never beaten by a climb'. What a year it had been: three amazing trips and 54 climbs in the bag. Roll on 2020.

All started well, plans were made for the year and the first trip was to check out the climbs around Calp and Valencia with Paul and Nick Burton. Something though was brewing on Planet Earth. Covid was starting to take hold and there was a nervousness in the air during our five-day trip which finished with us packing our bike bags with toilet paper because the shelves had been cleaned out

The only mountains I saw for two years were drawn on the wall in the back garden.

back home. We landed back in the UK just days before the world shut down and the project was well and truly put on ice.

No mountains were ridden of any sort for two whole years. I was desperate to get climbing again. Thankfully, in the spring of 2022 and after an experience that changed all our lives, it was game on once more.

With 64 in the bag, I had 36 to ride, spread between Gran Canaria, Cataluña, and central and southern Spain. The trip to Gran Canaria followed the same plan as our family week in Mallorca; one base with a great pool close to the beach where the family were very happy as I set off to bag my targets. What wasn't the same, was the climbs: Gran Canaria is Mallorca on steroids. This was no relaxing week trundling up shallow inclines like on its Mediterranean cousin; this island packs a serious punch with some brutal roads and not an inch of flat. I loved it! If you stay on the southern coast you can ride a smorgasbord of massive climbs all set in year-round warm air and absolutely pack your legs with altitude.

Just a couple of weeks later – and doing nothing for my carbon footprint – I was flying off again, this time to visit Cataluña and of course fashionable Girona. However, we chose to stay not in Girona, but in the far quieter town of Banyoles just to the north. You would struggle to find a better base for a few days riding anywhere. Offering everything from giant climbs to glorious flat roads and a myriad of tracks and trails, it's no wonder that this area is

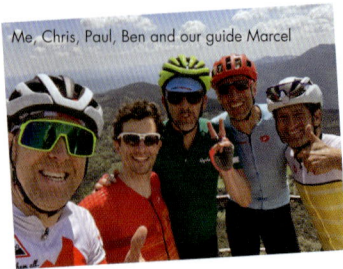
Me, Chris, Paul, Ben and our guide Marcel

so popular with people wanting a two-wheeled holiday.

There were four of us on this trip, and joining me were Paul, Ben Lowe of VeloViewer fame and 'young' Chris Moores who was there to put us all to the sword and chase some KOMs that our older legs could not get close to. By chance, we'd booked an Airbnb owned by one of Spain's greatest ever triathletes, Marcel Zamora. He was and still is an incredible athlete, and he graciously came out with us for a day to show us around the place he calls home.

With another nine climbs bagged, that just left one more adventure: a mammoth two-week trek with the family driving from Sheffield to the Med and back, clocking up 4,200 miles in the process to see one hell of a lot of Spain. Heading down via the Basque Country then settling in Segovia to tick off the Sierra de Guadarrama before crossing the wilds of La Mancha to reach the coast, the whole trip was undertaken during one of the hottest periods Europe has ever experienced. With daily temps hardly dropping below 30 degrees and peaking well in to the 40s, on some days this made riding a little challenging. Also, as

it didn't get light until 7 a.m., I'd have to be in the saddle, clipped in at my location as soon as the sun rose so that I could ride in whatever constituted cool air. Anything after 11 was horrendous, and that one day I decided to set off late afternoon, I was like a lobster in a pot being boiled alive. But these experiences are what make holidays, and one such experience topped them all and pretty much any I'd previously had – my ride up to Pico Veleta.

This was the BIG ONE. Forty kilometres of climbing (it would have been further if I'd started from Granada), a colossal ride which would see me heading upwards for over three hours. There are many combinations of roads you can link together to build your journey to the top and I had settled on a route which started in Pinos Genil on a back road then joined the main road a while later for its next stretch. As I joined the larger carriageway, I straight away noticed a line of cones on the right-hand side and as I continued it transpired that I was sharing the road that day with the Subida Al Pico Veleta. An annual marathon that's ALL uphill, it starts in Granada and finishes at 3,350

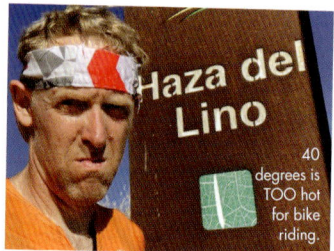

Pico Veleta. Gravel riding at over 3,300 metres altitude.

metres. INSANE.

My attempt to cycle to the top suddenly felt a little inadequate, but still, it would be a challenge, and arriving in Hoya de la Mora I still had almost 10 kilometres to go. I'd read various accounts about the condition of the road past the small ski village and was prepared for it to deteriorate significantly right away but was pleasantly surprised to find it still in rather good condition. In fact, for over seven kilometres through countless hairpins, all was going well. Soon enough though, holes started to appear … then bigger holes … then patches of gravel. Yes, I only had thin tyres (pumped up pretty hard), but I could handle some gravel, and anyway it was all the rage in 2022. The surface was still not completely broken either, and if I searched I could find patches of smooth, but entering the final bends things took a turn for the worse. There was now no more sealed road and the gravel, which had been just about rideable, was quickly turning to rubble. Of course, I had a desire to reach the top, but I also had a desire not to walk and wreck my new shoes, so I made the call to stop. I debated with my conscience for a good while and although I could see the summit from where I was standing, it would be some trek, so I threw in the towel. What a sensational place it was to stand, though. Over 500 metres higher than I had ever ridden before, it was like looking down on the Earth from space, the plains below little more than blue haze. UNFORGETTABLE.

So, that was it, almost. I bagged a couple more on the long drive back north, and we had one last blowout in our favourite city of Donostia, a wrap party for what had been an almost-eight-year project, before returning to our cold island in the North Sea.

What adventures, what roads, and here they are all bound in these 240 pages. I hope this book helps you plan your trips and hope you find these amazing roads as breathtaking as I did. There are some simply astonishing sights to be seen across the wonderful country of Spain and many monumental challenges to be undertaken.

Have fun, Simon.

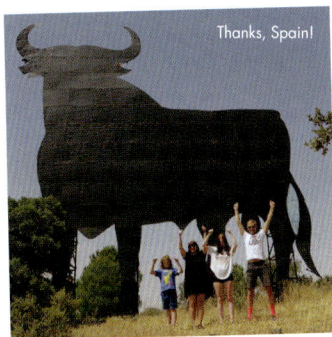
Thanks, Spain!

How to use the book

FACTFILE

DIRECTIONS: Head north-west out of Palma on Camino de Gènova then begin ~~t~~ ~~rough the two~~ ro~~~~ ~~~~e MA-20.

SU~~~~ 380m
HE~~~~ 302m
MAXI~~~~ 10%
AVERAGE GRADIENT 5.2%

THE FACT FILE TELLS YOU HOW TO FIND THE START OF EACH CLIMB AND LISTS ITS VITAL STATISTICS

THE PROFILE GIVES YOU A SNAPSHOT OF THE CLIMB TOGETHER WITH ITS LENGTH

HERE IS THE APPROXIMATE PLACE WHERE YOU'LL FIND THE STEEPEST GRADIENT ON THE CLIMB

MAX GRADIENT
10%

5.8km

100

0   1   2   3   4   5km

MA-1110
ESPORLES
MA-1120   MA-1~~~~
PALMA DE MALLORCA
MA-20
MA-1

THE SMALL MAP SHOWS THE PREMIUM ROUTE IN YELLOW WITH OTHER RECOGNISED ROUTES IN BLACK

MA-1043
MA-1016
PALMA DE MALLORCA
MA-20
MA-1044
GÈNOVA
MA-1
MA-1

THE LARGER MAP ILLUSTRATES THE ROUTE LOCATION IN MORE DETAIL

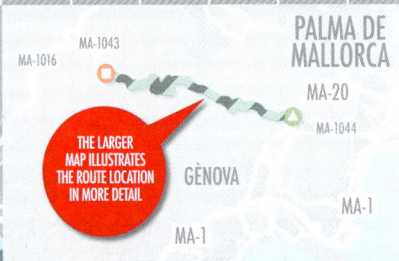

LOCATIONS

On each page you will find two maps: one showing the area the climb sits in and another that pinpoints the exact route. Although you should be able to locate each hill using these, I would always recommend you take a comprehensive map of the area or a GPS/satnav device to cross-reference.

RATINGS

The climbs are rated within the context of the book. The rating is an amalgamation of gradient, length, the likely hostility of the riding conditions and the quality of the surface. All the climbs are tough, therefore 1/10 equals 'hard', and 10/10 equals 'almost impossible'.

10/10

KEY TO THE MAPS

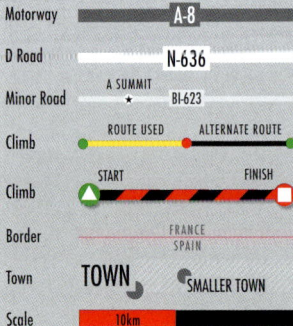

Motorway	A-8
D Road	N-636
Minor Road	A SUMMIT ★ BI-623
Climb	ROUTE USED ALTERNATE ROUTE
Climb	START FINISH
Border	FRANCE / SPAIN
Town	TOWN ● SMALLER TOWN
Scale	10km

!

WARNING

One last thing before we get started. While it may be 30 degrees Celsius in the valley, that doesn't mean it won't be snowing at the top! So always, ALWAYS take a jacket. Now, to the mountains!

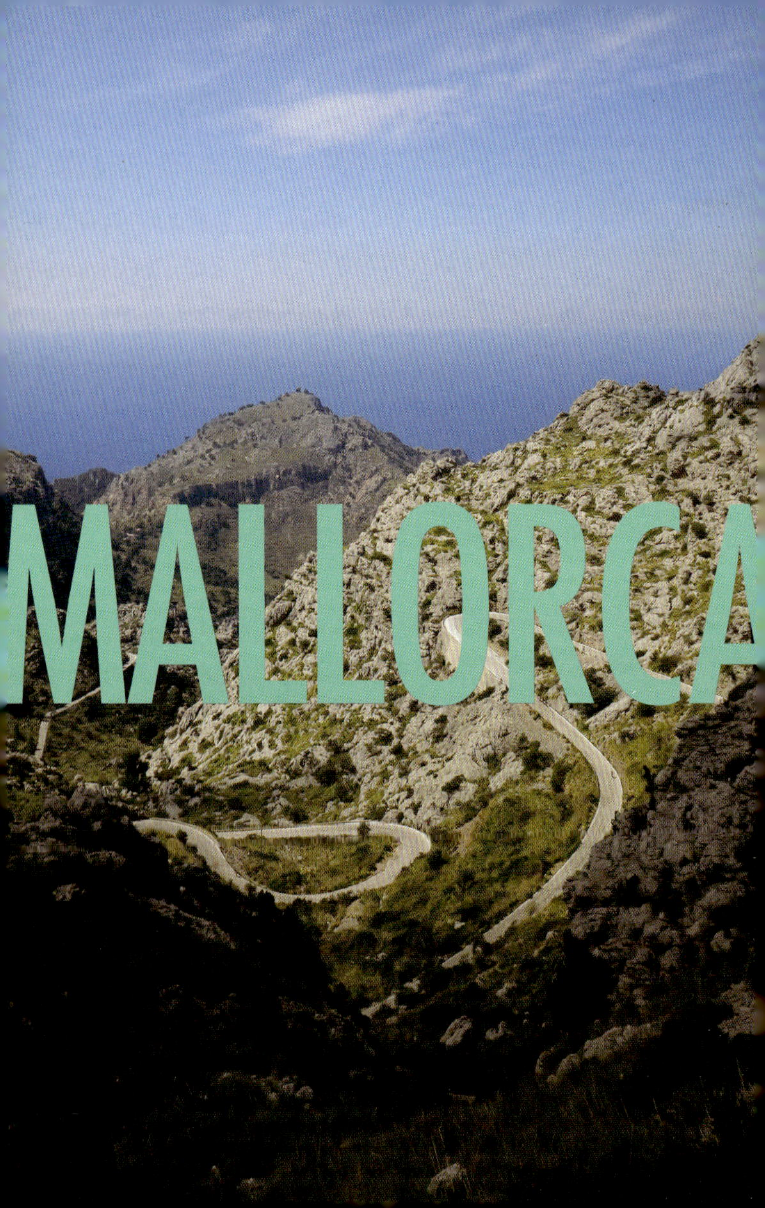
MALLORCA

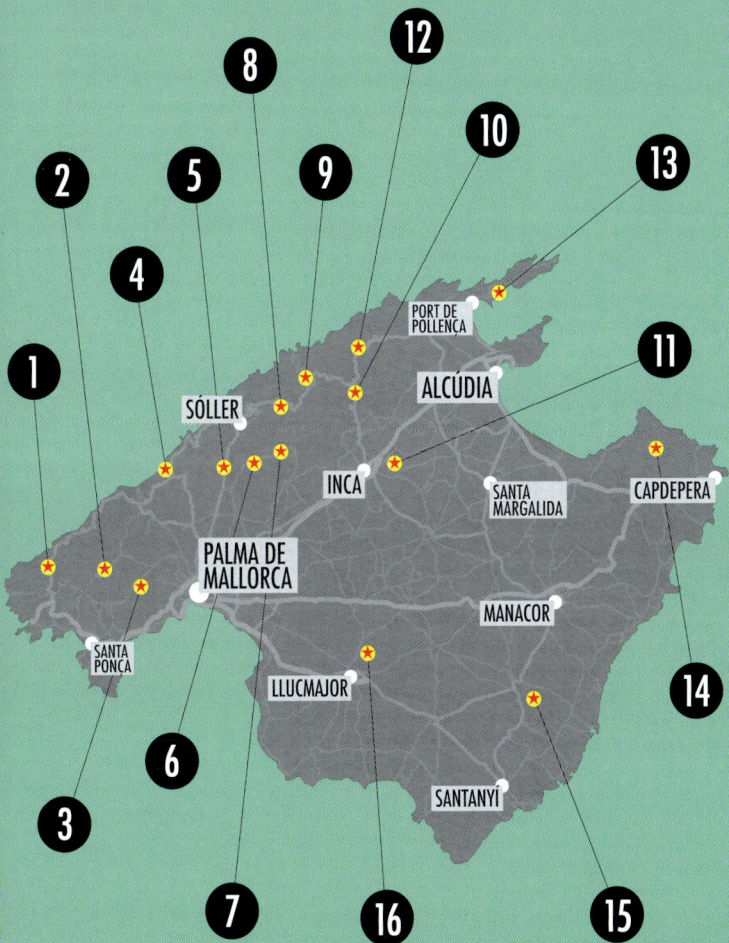

MEDITERRANEAN
SEA

PORT DE POLLENÇA

ALCÚDIA

SÓLLER

INCA

SANTA MARGALIDA

CAPDEPERA

PALMA DE MALLORCA

MANACOR

SANTA PONÇA

LLUCMAJOR

SANTANYÍ

1 Coll de sa Gramola

Rising out of Anthrax … sorry, Andratx, the Coll de sa Gramola kicks off the amazing road that traces Mallorca's north coast all the way to Sóller. Flirting with the shore and offering exquisite views out over the waves before diving back inland to snake through the rugged interior, this almost-impossibly smooth tarmac is cycling nirvana. The base lies in the north-east corner of Andratx where the MA-10 rises away from a roundabout following the signs to Sóller. Beneath a partial covering of trees and lined with outcrops of jagged red rock, the early slopes are reasonably hard as they approach 8%. After almost a kilometre of this gradient the climb calms down and the rest of the ascent is set on a very agreeable 5% slope. Winding effortlessly upwards, this immaculate monument to road building is asphalt fine art, such is its perfection. As the trees fade, the landscape opens to reveal a sparsely vegetated, almost terracotta-coloured landscape populated by a series of rocky peaks. Then the summit approaches – you'll spy the road bisecting the hillside and once through this miniature canyon there's a lay-by where you can pause to soak up the views before continuing north on this highway from heaven.

FACTFILE

DIRECTIONS: From the north-east corner of Andratx begin on the Carretera de Estellencs (MA-10) leaving the roundabout at the junction with the MA-1031.

SUMMIT ALTITUDE	361 m
HEIGHT GAIN	282 m
MAXIMUM GRADIENT	8%
AVERAGE GRADIENT	5.5%

MAX GRADIENT
8%

5.2km

300m

200

100

0   1   2   3   4   5km

MA-10

ANDRATX

MA-1

PORT D'ANDRATX

PEGUERA

MA-1

SANTA PONÇA

10km

S'ARRACÓ

MA-1030

MA-1031

SA COMA

ES CAPDELLÀ

ANDRATX

MA-1

MA-1012

2 Es Capdellà

There are two climbs on the road that links Es Capdellà with Esporles to the north, passing through Galilea and Puigpunyent en route. Both climbs are well worth the ride, but I've only documented one here and it was a tough choice between the two. Taking its name from the town at the bottom, Es Capdellà got the nod as, of the two climbs ridden in either direction, it features a winning combination of length and gradient. Rolling out of town on the MA-1032 in the direction of Galilea, the climb proper doesn't kick in until you pass through the river basin after almost three kilometres. From here, the transition to climbing is almost immediate as the road bends right and heads upwards. Set predominantly on a 5–6% slope, the first three kilometres are a relative breeze as the road, carved out of the red earth and lined with outcrops of vivid orange stone, meanders up the hillside. As you close in on Galilea, the gradient does start to kick up and there are some much tougher sections to tackle as stone walls start to replace the rocks at the sides of the road and agriculture begins to populate the hillsides. The summit lies in the dead centre of the village, from where you roll down immediately to carry on to Puigpunyent and the base of the next climb.

FACTFILE

DIRECTIONS: Head east from Es Capdellà on the MA-1032 and start to climb after roughly three kilometres.

SUMMIT ALTITUDE	413m
HEIGHT GAIN	279m
MAXIMUM GRADIENT	10%
AVERAGE GRADIENT	5.9%

MAX GRADIENT
10%

400m
300
200
0

4.7km

0   1   2   3   4km

MA-10

ANDRATX
MA-1

PORT
D'ANDRATX   PEGUERA

SANTA
PONÇA

10km

GALILEA   MA-1032

MA-1031

SA COMA   MA-1032

ES CAPDELLÀ

3 Coll des Vent

If you're starting your ride in Palma, just take care while exiting the city as the larger roads can be somewhat intimidating for the diminutive cyclist. Once across the MA-20 ring road, however, the transition from metropolis to nature is almost instant as you head north-west into the mountains. The first couple of kilometres are far from pretty as the road undulates past an army base and through more agricultural land, but all that changes once you enter the forest. With an increase in gradient, the now much narrower road begins to swirl through the landscape, this way and that, picking its course upwards. As bare rock begins to protrude from the red earth, you'll maybe have to click down a couple of gears, but the slope is never too steep. Like the majority of Mallorcan forest roads, the surface is impeccable, faultless, a magic carpet of sublime asphalt fragranced by the surrounding pines. Honestly, if this road went on forever, you'd never get bored, but I'm afraid it must end, and you reach the summit just shy of the six-kilometre mark. The road immediately descends, on a similarly mild slope, down the other side to continue your journey through cycling paradise.

FACTFILE

DIRECTIONS: Head north-west out of Palma on Camino de Gènova then begin to climb once through the two roundabouts across the MA-20.

SUMMIT ALTITUDE	380m
HEIGHT GAIN	302m
MAXIMUM GRADIENT	10%
AVERAGE GRADIENT	5.2%

MAX GRADIENT **10%**

5.8km

300m
200
100
0

1 2 3 4 5km

MA-10
MA-1110
ESPORLES
MA-1120
MA-11
PALMA DE MALLORCA
MA-20
MA-1
10km

MA-1016
MA-1043
MA-20
MA-1044
PALMA DE MALLORCA
GÈNOVA
MA-1
MA-1

4 Port de Valldemossa

You will all have heard of Sa Calobra (page 35), but how many of you are familiar with this amazing climb, which, to coin a popular phrase, is 'Sa Calobra on steroids'? The premise is the same: a twisting, writhing road that leads down to a small harbour, but instead of being filled with coachloads of tourists, this hidden gem is as quiet as a mouse, oh, and *much* steeper! Just like its more famous peer, you descend first so you can get a good look at what you're in for on your journey back up, and believe me it will leave you feeling slightly nervous. There's a small restaurant at the harbour where you can refuel, but I'd advise against a large meal as it will certainly weigh heavy as you set off to tackle an average gradient of 8% over 4.9 kilometres. Packed with 10 vicious hairpins where the gradient tips up well into double figures, this climb feels much tougher than the average suggests. Back and forth, with fleeting glimpses out over the sea, you zigzag up the steep hillside beneath the conifers. The instant I laid eyes on this road I knew it would become my favourite Mallorcan climb, and once at the top my initial reaction was confirmed. It is an absolutely classic road, barely wide enough for a single car, and packed with tight hairpins and glorious views. It is every bit the equal of Sa Calobra!

FACTFILE

DIRECTIONS: Head west out of Valldemossa on the MA-10 then turn north on to the MA-1131 to descend all the way to the shore before turning to climb back up.

SUMMIT ALTITUDE	373m
HEIGHT GAIN	369m
MAXIMUM GRADIENT	15%
AVERAGE GRADIENT	7.4%

MAX GRADIENT
15%

4.9km

300m
200
100
0   1   2   3   4km

MA-10
MA-11
SÓLLER

PORT DE VALLDEMOSSA

MA-10

VALLDEMOSSA

MA-1131

VALLDEMOSSA

VALLDEMOSSA
MA-1110

MA-10

ESPORLES
MA-1120
MA-11

MA-1110

10km

5 Coll de Sóller

Of the two ways up the Coll de Sóller, this one, the north face, is in my opinion the best. The southern flank, while boasting an outrageous 22 hairpins crammed into just five kilometres, just isn't quite as challenging. From the north, the ascent starts as you pass through the final roundabout heading south from Sóller on the MA-11. The first two kilometres lie in a dead-straight line and are pretty busy, but where the majority of traffic heads straight on into the tunnel, you turn left and the real fun begins. Whereas the south side has 22 hairpins, this side has 29 and they come at you with such frequency it's enough to make you dizzy. Back and forth you thrash up the mountainside, in and out of the saddle and up and down the gears to cope with the constant changes in gradient around the bends. Each time you turn south you catch a glimpse of the view down the valley, then each time you flip back north the horizon moves a little closer. The tougher gradients are all to be found lower down, and as you approach the peak you can really pick up some speed to finish with a flourish before the exhilarating technical descent over the other side.

FACTFILE

DIRECTIONS: Head south out of Sóller on the MA-11 and start to climb from the final roundabout then turn left as the main road heads into the tunnel.

SUMMIT ALTITUDE	497m
HEIGHT GAIN	452m
MAXIMUM GRADIENT	10%
AVERAGE GRADIENT	5.9%

MAX GRADIENT **10%**

7.6km

6 Coll d'Honor

Cutting through the interior of the Tramuntana mountains, the Coll d'Honor links Bunyola with the Orient valley. A much harder test heading east, the climb leaves Bunyola on the MA-2100 tracing the flow of the small river to its left. The base is hidden in the narrow streets of the village where you leave Calle Major heading north up and through a pair of tight, steep bends. Continue away from the houses and soon you are immersed in the lush valley surrounded by green mountain peaks on both sides. This climb isn't littered with hairpins – they are few and far between and the first appear with roughly two kilometres covered. Apart from brief spikes of double-digit gradient around the smattering of tight bends, the slope sticks reliably to a moderate 5% incline to allow you to make good progress. There are no grand views as you're trapped for most of the ascent in the forest, which does have the benefit of offering a decent amount of shade on hotter days. Finishing with a flourish through a quick succession of five tightly packed bends and some slightly stiffer gradient, the summit arrives with little fanfare at the side of the small brown sign.

FACTFILE

DIRECTIONS: From Bunyola, head east on Calle Major then turn left across the small plaza to leave its north-east corner on Carrer Rector Rullan, the MA-2100.

SUMMIT ALTITUDE	550m
HEIGHT GAIN	340m
MAXIMUM GRADIENT	12%
AVERAGE GRADIENT	5.8%

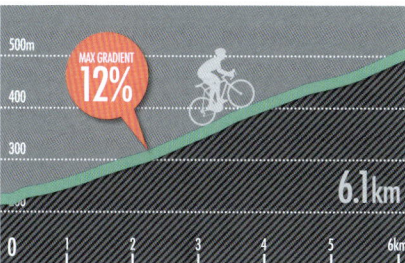

MAX GRADIENT **12%**

6.1km

7 Col de Orient

Heading into the Orient valley, which lies hidden away in the Serra de Tramuntana, the Col d'Orient is five kilometres of 5% gradient on a five-star road surface. Linking Alaró with Orient, and ultimately Bunyola via the Coll d'Honor, this road is immaculate from start to finish. Dropping out the back of Alaró, the climb begins ever so gently as you hit the valley floor, then gradually starts to tip upwards as you approach the hills ahead. Leaving farmland behind, you rise into the mountains beneath towering rust-coloured buttes on either side, their vertical rock faces standing like monuments on top of the green peaks. Beneath your wheels all is calm and serene as the mild gradient – without the complication of bends – embarks on its giant left-hand arc. As the road completes its turn west, tremendous views over the high mountain peaks are revealed across the valley as you make your push for the finish. If you're feeling brave, or aided by a nice tailwind, you'll be tempted to big-ring it towards the top (that is if you aren't already) to rapidly tick off the final kilometre to the summit sign that lies just shy of the village of Orient.

FACTFILE

DIRECTIONS: Leave the north of Alaró on Carretera de Alaró a Bunyola, the MA-2100, following the signs to Orient and Bunyola.

SUMMIT ALTITUDE	498m
HEIGHT GAIN	275m
MAXIMUM GRADIENT	8%
AVERAGE GRADIENT	3.6%

MAX GRADIENT
8%

7.6km

400m

300

MALLORCA

This, the longest climb on the island, Mallorca's MAJOR ascent, was, to be honest, something of a disappointment to me. Its billing as the island's highest pass, with the promise of endless hairpins and stunning views, had the hairs on the back of my neck tingling with excitement. Although, yes, there were plenty of twists and turns, the views were a bit of a let-down, as was the mild nature of the gradient. Having said all that, it's still a cracking road to climb, and, with an average slope below 6% and a maximum of just 8%, it's never a chore. Leaving L'Horta to the north of Sóller, the 'official' start lies at the junction of the MA-11 and MA-10. Turning east you begin by weaving past houses then soon you're into the wonderful wooded hillsides. With barely any change in surroundings along its entire length, the road metronomically swings left and right, easing up the mountainside. With a perpetual wall of bare rock on one side and intermittent glimpses out over the island on the other, you can tick off the kilometres with relative ease. The rock arch at just over halfway acts as a good landmark to help you gauge your effort to the summit, which lies just before the very dark tunnel that takes you over the crest.

FACTFILE

DIRECTIONS: Start the climb in L'Horta north of Sóller by heading east on the MA-10 away from the junction with the MA-11.

SUMMIT ALTITUDE	871m
HEIGHT GAIN	840m
MAXIMUM GRADIENT	8%
AVERAGE GRADIENT	5.8%

MAX GRADIENT **8%**

14.4km

Perfect. Utterly perfect. Well, almost. The first tip for riding Sa Calobra is get there early, especially if it's your intention to put down a fast time, because by mid-morning the coaches will be starting to arrive, ferrying tourists to the fishing village at the bottom. Blocking the hairpins and polluting the air, they are annoying, but without them and the visitors they carry we would not have what is regarded by many as the ultimate cycling climb. Just shy of ten kilometres long, this magnificent tangle of tarmac twists its way from shore to sky through the simply exquisite rocky landscape. To ride it you must of course descend first, so on your way down you can marvel at its beauty and the genius of its construction. Then, after arriving at the base, turn right round and smash it back up. Almost faultless from start to finish, there are two more features, one natural and one man-made, that embellish the road even further. First, after two kilometres, you come to the famous narrowing as the road squeezes between two giant rock faces. Then, within a kilometre of the summit, you reach the 360-degree corner where the road loops round and passes over itself before the final push for the summit, which, to be geographically correct, is the Coll dels Reis. Enjoy!

FACTFILE

DIRECTIONS: Head north from the junction of the MA-10 and MA-2141. Climb up and over the Coll dels Reis, drop down the other side then turn round and GO!

SUMMIT ALTITUDE	723m
HEIGHT GAIN	667m
MAXIMUM GRADIENT	11%
AVERAGE GRADIENT	6.9%

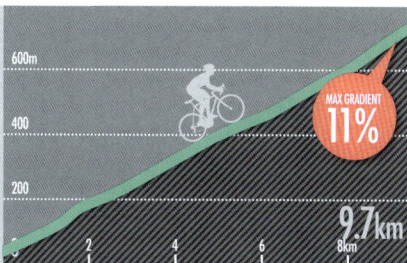

MAX GRADIENT **11%**

9.7km

SA CALOBRA

SA CALOBRA

MA-10

SÓLLER

MA-2141

MA-10

SON MACIP

MA-10

10 Coll de sa Batalla

The summit of the Coll de sa Batalla sits at the midpoint of the MA-10 which runs north-east–south-west through the Serra de Tramuntana. A long climb by Mallorcan standards at over eight kilometres in length, it is however anything but tough; a good example of what you might label a perfect beginners' climb. Leaving the plains at Caimari, the road rises into the mountains and it's not long before it starts to thrash back and forth through the first of three groups of hairpins. Wide and never too steep, the luscious tarmac heads north between the thinly vegetated peaks. The higher you climb, ever-more bare rock protrudes from the landscape, topped with gnarled conifers and surrounded by a carpet of needles and terracotta earth. As you approach the final set of hairpins, the road is freed from the forest and, passing through a giant cleft in the mountain, the views are outstanding. Dramatic enough to halt your progress, in fact, so it's more than acceptable to take a break here before heading into the next jumble of six tightly packed corners where at last some tougher gradients can be found. Once out of these, there remains just the final push to the summit where you'll find a garage and on any given day a café heaving with fellow riders.

FACTFILE

DIRECTIONS: Head north out of Selva on the MA-2130, drop down to the flat plains then begin to climb as you reach Caimari following the signs to Sa Calobra.

SUMMIT ALTITUDE	576m
HEIGHT GAIN	403m
MAXIMUM GRADIENT	12%
AVERAGE GRADIENT	4.9%

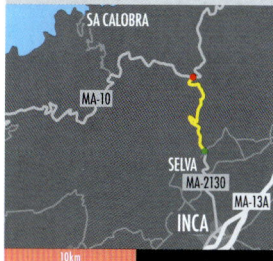

MAX GRADIENT 12%

8.3km

11 Puig de Santa Magdalena

The climbs in Mallorca can be split into two types. Those in the mountainous north of the island, and then ones like this that snake up the small, isolated hills that protrude from the predominantly flat lands to the south. All topped with a sanctuary or chapel of some description, they make fantastic diversions to test your climbing legs and to take in the awesome views they facilitate. I visited six such peaks, and of those six, three made the cut, the first of which is this, the Puig de Santa Magdalena. Located just east of Inca, this rocky protrusion punctuates the otherwise-flat horizon so the base isn't too hard to locate on the Camino Viejo de Santa Magdalena. From here, you turn south on the long, straight and slightly inclined approach to the left-hand bend where you start to gain altitude with more rapidity. On its hairpin-laden trek to the summit through nine tight corners, the far-from-savage slope cuts across the tree-littered hillside on an increasingly narrow road. As with all the vertical deformations on the island's flat lands, the views are instantly dramatic and only improve the higher you climb, so keep the pressure on the pedals until you reach the very top. Over the final 400 metres the slope relaxes significantly to allow you to click up a couple of gears in the final push to the restaurant with a view to die for.

FACTFILE

DIRECTIONS: Head south-east from Inca on Avenida de los Reis Catòlics, turn left on to the Camino Viejo de Santa Magdalena over the MA-13, then turn south to climb.

SUMMIT ALTITUDE	289m
HEIGHT GAIN	174m
MAXIMUM GRADIENT	14%
AVERAGE GRADIENT	6.4%

MAX GRADIENT 14%

2.7km

12 Coll de Femenia

Not another perfectly smooth road set on a sublime 5% gradient that winds up through pristine scenery, you say? Well, sorry, I'm afraid so. It's easy to see why Mallorca is so popular with cyclists of all abilities with roads like this on the island; it is utterly without fault on all levels. To find the base, head west from Pollença on the MA-10 and after almost dead-on six kilometres of pan-flat riding the gradient starts to bite. Not bite like a great white shark though, more like a playful puppy with rubber teeth. Ever so slightly it ramps up, easing you into the climbing like you'd ease an elderly relative into their favourite comfy chair. Before long you pass through the climb's only real hairpins as the road navigates through the sparse covering of trees that protrude from the landscape of exposed rock. Revealing spellbinding views out over the Serra de Tramuntana, you pierce the heart of the mountains, weaving higher in search of the summit. Before you reach the top, the road undulates a little, allowing you to click through the gears and pick up some speed, then once over the top it's time to continue for a date with Sa Calobra!

FACTFILE

DIRECTIONS: Simply head west from Pollença on the MA-10 and keep going until you start to climb.

SUMMIT ALTITUDE	538m
HEIGHT GAIN	438m
MAXIMUM GRADIENT	8%
AVERAGE GRADIENT	5.2%

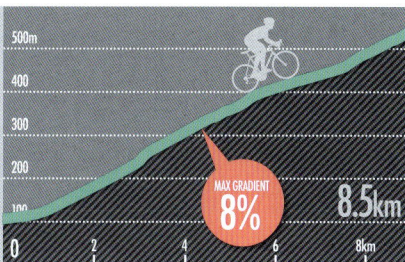

MAX GRADIENT
8%

8.5km

13 Talaia d'Albercutx

One destination all riders have on their Mallorca bucket list is the 'climb' to the Formentor lighthouse. This most beautiful of roads that weaves along the peninsula jutting out from the north-eastern corner of the island, is however NOT a climb, not in my book; it has far too many ups and downs to be a true ascent. But, from the same start point as you begin your journey to the end of the island, there IS a proper climb. Leaving Port de Pollença, begin the ascent from the roundabout and head directly into a pair of hairpins on the MA-2210. For the first 3.3 kilometres you rise gradually on a 6% slope to the bar at the summit of the Coll de sa Creueta, but instead of rolling over the top towards the lighthouse, you turn right for some serious action. Ahead, you will see the the road traversing the hillside like a miniature Great Wall of China. The feel of the climb changes instantly, and it's now very narrow, rough and far quieter. On the whole, the gradient sticks to a sensible 7–8%, but in places there are some far more demanding spikes as the narrow road which teeters on the edge of the peak snakes to the watchtower at the summit where you can take in views across stunning azure waters on both sides.

FACTFILE

DIRECTIONS: From the north-east corner over Port de Pollença start the climb at the roundabout on the MA-2210

SUMMIT ALTITUDE	365m
HEIGHT GAIN	353m
MAXIMUM GRADIENT	18%
AVERAGE GRADIENT	6.2%

14 Coll de sa Millera

Winding its way to the secluded monastery in the mountains, I found the climb to Ermita de Betlem to be one of the quietest on the island. Hidden in the heart of the Parc Natural de la Península de Llevant, it is achingly beautiful from start to finish as you cut through this haven for both flora and fauna. Leaving Artà, you need to travel north for a few kilometres along the flat before the slope starts to bite as the road begins its ascent through olive groves and past the odd farmhouse. Following the early gentle forays, you're next afforded close to a kilometre on the flat before the climbing then starts once more as the bends arrive. Twisting into the Artà mountains, the vegetation is typically sparse yet unusually varied as immersed in natural beauty the narrow ribbon of immaculate tarmac picks its way upwards. With some sharp spikes in gradient through the tighter corners, it then levels slightly before the summit where the views are, as to be expected, exceptional. You have not yet reached the sanctuary however, so if you wish to do this you must first drop over the other side for 1,500 metres before making a U-turn. Which of course means you are treated to another 1,500 metres of glorious climbing on the way home. Bonus!

FACTFILE

DIRECTIONS: Head north from Artà on the MA-3333 past the Palacio Sant Salvador then start to climb just after the fork following the sign to the ermita.

SUMMIT ALTITUDE	374m
HEIGHT GAIN	233m
MAXIMUM GRADIENT	17%
AVERAGE GRADIENT	4.5%

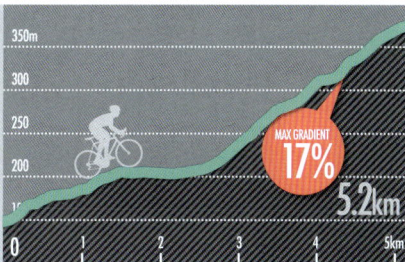

MAX GRADIENT **17%**

5.2km

MA-12 ARTÀ MA-15 CAPDEPERA

MA-15

10km

MA-3333

ARTÀ

MA-12 MA-15

MA-4042

15 Puig de San Salvador

This little climb is the star of south-east Mallorca and is well worth the trip from the more-favoured north of the island. Hugely popular with both cyclists and tourists visiting the monastery at the top, if you want a clear ride then I recommend you head out early to avoid the hordes. Located in the diminutive Llevant mountains that run down the eastern side of the island, you'll spy its peak as you leave the MA-4010 just east of Felanitx to start the ascent. The climb kicks up almost as soon as you exit the main road with the first kilometre rising in a dead-straight line. Then, after the uniformity of the early slope, the bends start to arrive, gently at first but the higher you climb the more tightly packed and contorted they become. With spikes in gradient that touch 15% and an average of close to 7%, this is one of the toughest climbs on the island, even if it is only 4.7 kilometres long. In regular use as a summit finish in races, you'll see the names of riders daubed across the tarmac higher up - that is if you can keep your eyes off the dazzling views that surround you. Snaking around the peak up to the base of the imposing sanctuary, the gradient fades to deliver you to a café that simply demands a stop so you can soak in more of the wonderful vista.

FACTFILE

DIRECTIONS: Leave Felanitx on the MA-4010 then take the right hand turn which is marked by rather elaborate walls and follow the sign to Sant Salvador.

SUMMIT ALTITUDE	494m
HEIGHT GAIN	325m
MAXIMUM GRADIENT	15%
AVERAGE GRADIENT	6.8%

MAX GRADIENT
15%

400m
300
200

4.7km

0   1   2   3   4km

MA-14
FELANITX
MA-5120
CALES DE MALLORCA
MA-14
PORTOCOLOM
CALA D'OR
MA-19

10km

MA-14
MA-5120
FELANITX
MA-4010
MA-14

16 Puig de Randa

If you want epic views of Mallorca, forget about Puig Major and the climbs in the north and head directly here to the Puig de Randa. Of all the small, isolated hills that pop up from the southern flat lands, it's this little gem that boasts the grandest vista. The climb itself is not especially pretty and the summit is cluttered by a carbuncle of radio masts and associated dilapidated buildings, but the views are just breathtaking. You start the ascent in the tiny village of Randa by following the signs to the Santuari de Cura. Before long you'll pass the last building and begin the first part of the climb heading east before it turns north into the tangle of hairpins. With only a 5% average, this road is no killer, although there are a few patches of harsher slope, especially in the sharp corners. As you cross the scrubby bush-covered scenery when you reach the change in direction, the first views appear, and barely halfway up they are already impressive. Improving all the way whenever you catch sight of them, you keep climbing to the final hairpin where the gradient all but vanishes. You're not at the top yet but the hard work is done, so now you just need to press on past the telecommunications paraphernalia to the gates to the sanctuary from where you can cast your eyes out over the whole island.

FACTFILE

DIRECTIONS: Head south-east through Randa on Calle de la Creu, then from the crossroads head up the MA-5018 following the sign to Santuari de Cura.

SUMMIT ALTITUDE	541 m
HEIGHT GAIN	252 m
MAXIMUM GRADIENT	8%
AVERAGE GRADIENT	5.3%

MAX GRADIENT **8%**

4.8km

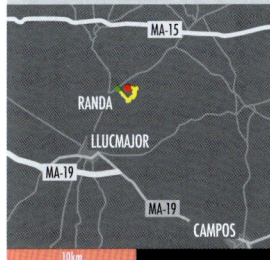

MA-15

RANDA

LLUCMAJOR

MA-19

MA-19

CAMPOS

MA-5010

MA-5017

MA-5010

RANDA

MA-5010

NORTHE

ATLANTIC
OCEAN

LA CORUÑA

SANTIAGO DE
COMPOSTELA

38

35

34

32

42

GIJÓN

OVIEDO

SAN

ASTURIAS

CAN

39

LUGO

41

GALICIA

44

43

40

36

33

ORENSE

PONFERRADA

LEÓN

31

45

37

PALENCIA

CASTILLA Y LEÓN

PORTUGAL

ZAMORA

VALLADO

RN SPAIN

FRANCE

28
23
24
25
22
19
29
20
18
17

BILBAO
SAN SEBASTIÁN

BASQUE
COUNTRY
VITORIA-
GASTEIZ
PAMPLONA

26
30
NAVARRA

27
LOGROÑO
BURGOS
LA RIOJA

HUESCA

21
ARAGÓN

LÉRIDA

ZARAGOZA

17 Puerto del Portalet

The Puerto del Portalet – or, in French, the Col du Pourtalet – links the Tena valley in Spain with the Ossau valley in France, and this ancient frontier crossing has been used many times in both the Tour de France and the Vuelta a España. The climbing begins in Biescas where the slope is really steady until you approach the town of Búbal. Here, there is a tough kilometre of 8% average which peaks close to 10%, before it subsides to pretty much run flat all the way past the large reservoir to Escarrilla. Now the climbing gets a touch more serious. Leaving town there is a tunnel to avoid by turning right at its entrance to take the short detour, and once you rejoin the main road you head up past another reservoir, rising again really gently between 3 and 5%. This is a very easy climb all told, however there are a couple of further hotspots of more demanding gradient to keep you working: the first after 19 kilometres, and the second after 23 kilometres. Turning north-west you pass the turn to the ski village of Formigal and the also many car parks that line the road at regular intervals. Cutting through the grand valley, tracing the course of the Río Gállego, you arrive at the summit and the border with France, which is marked with abandoned, decaying checkpoints.

FACTFILE

DIRECTIONS: Start by simply heading north out of Biescas on the A-136.

SUMMIT ALTITUDE	1794m
HEIGHT GAIN	929m
MAXIMUM GRADIENT	11%
AVERAGE GRADIENT	3.4%

MAX GRADIENT **11%**

26.9km

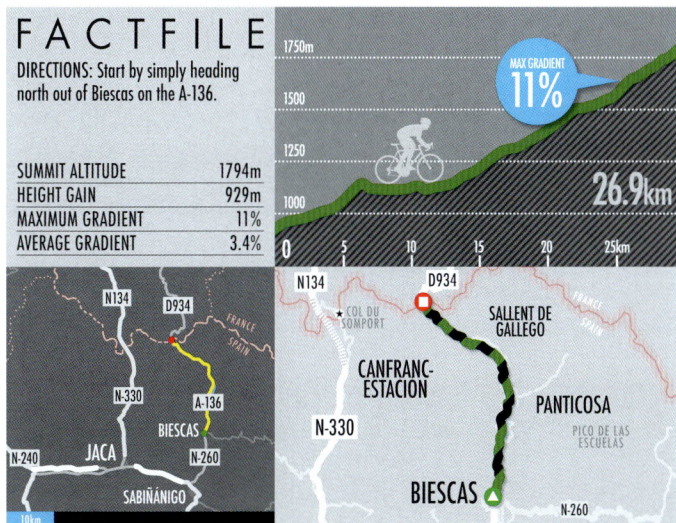

18 Collado de Piedra de San Martín

Linking Spain with France, this pass has a rather convoluted finish as it teases the border for some distance before eventually crossing it. A relatively remote road, you must travel north through Burgui, Roncal, Urzainqui and Isaba before you reach the base in the Reserva Natural de Larra. Crossing the Río Belagua, the NA-137 bends left and kicks up into eight kilometres of substantial climbing. Starting at around 6% but settling down on to a slope closer to 8%, it ramps up to and through a series of seven hairpins. Rising rapidly up the valley wall, once through the final tight bend the views are immense, but there is still a great deal of hard work ahead through the remaining three kilometres to the first brush with the border. Immersed in mountain scenery, the slope fades to all but level out as you begin to straddle the boundary with France, the road trading views left and right over the mighty Pyrenees. After this mid-climb hiatus, the final three kilometres to the summit are tough again; not quite as hard as the start though, as they weave through towering rocks searching for the border. Through a dramatic 360-degree loop where the road ties itself into a knot, you eventually – after a couple of false dawns – reach the ultimate summit, which lies not in Spain, but in France.

FACTFILE

DIRECTIONS: You must head north on the NA-137 through Burgui, Roncal, Urzainqui and Isaba before reaching the base as you cross the Río Belagua.

SUMMIT ALTITUDE	1760m
HEIGHT GAIN	782 m
MAXIMUM GRADIENT	9%
AVERAGE GRADIENT	5.4%

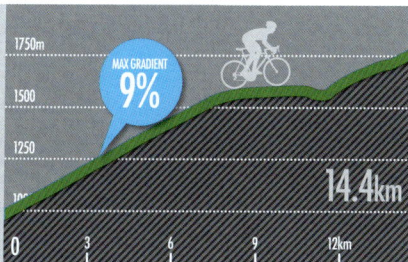

MAX GRADIENT **9%**

14.4km

19 Alto de Jaizkibel

Some climbs have a symbiotic relationship with the races in which they feature, and they are almost as famous as the races themselves. Think the Poggio at the end of Milan-San Remo, or the Madonna del Ghisallo on Il Lombardia, for example. This climb, the Alto de Jaizkibel, is another such incline as it features each year and plays a key part in deciding the outcome of the Donostia-Donostia Klasikoa (San Sebastián Classic). The ascent kicks off to the east of Donostia (San Sebastián) from the small town of Lezo and heads north on the GI-3440 into the mountains. The start is where the toughest gradients are to be found as the road rises into the hairpins through the forest, but what begins at around the 8% mark soon drops to a more manageable 6–7% slope. Through the four tight bends and you are soon free of the conifers and rising high above the Bay of Biscay. From here to the summit the views are almost constant over your left shoulder and only get better, as following a short levelling and slight drop the slope resumes hostilities on a 7% pitch. Closing in on the summit, the pitch starts to relax, allowing you to click up and up though the gears as you tick off the last couple of kilometres to finish only once you have passed the sign that marks the top.

FACTFILE

DIRECTIONS: Start the climb on the GI-3440 where it heads north from the T-junction following the signs to Jaizkibel.

SUMMIT ALTITUDE	455m
HEIGHT GAIN	451m
MAXIMUM GRADIENT	16%
AVERAGE GRADIENT	5.6%

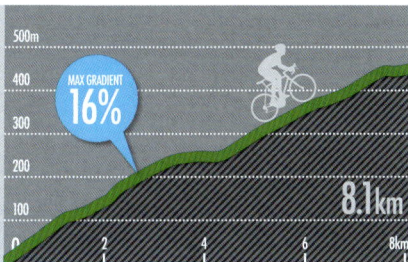

MAX GRADIENT
16%

8.1km

BAY OF BISCAY

SAN SEBASTIÁN

HONDARRIBIA
AP-8
FRANCE

AP-8

ANDOAIN
A-15

N-121A

ORDIZIA
N-1
A-15

10km

BAY OF BISCAY

GI-3440

TRINTXERPE
GI-636

LEZO

SAGASTI
GI-636

LINTZIRIN
AP-8

ERRENTERIA

A very agreeable climb with no hidden horrors, just pure climbing pleasure. You start by heading south from Etxarri-Aranatz, over the motorway and into the valley. The first couple of kilometres are all but flat before the initially negligible gradient eventually steepens slightly into Lizarraga. You'll know you're climbing now as you exit the hillside village via two sweeping hairpins. Faced with a wall of rock ahead, your eyes will begin to search for a possible path through this seemingly impenetrable barrier. Meandering as the road climbs, there are only three hairpins now between you and the summit, and they are placed far apart – three colossal corners that split the ascent. After the slightly aggressive 6–8% slope out of Lizarraga, the road soon settles into the 5% incline that it holds the rest of the way to the top. The views out across to the Sierra de Andía mountains come and go as you dive in and out of the trees that line the road, but when you get a clear line of sight, they are enough to stop you in your tracks. Riding into the Urbasa y Andía Natural Park which houses the southern face of the climb, to reach the true summit you must pass through a short, unlit tunnel carved straight out of the mountain.

FACTFILE

DIRECTIONS: Leave Aranatz heading south-east on the NA-120 up and over the motorway bridge then start the climb as it rises out of the valley.

SUMMIT ALTITUDE	1031m
HEIGHT GAIN	545m
MAXIMUM GRADIENT	8%
AVERAGE GRADIENT	5%

MAX GRADIENT
8%

11km

21 Lagunas de Neila

Situated far from any other climb in this book, which will no doubt inconvenience completists keen to ride them all, it was essential to include this one as it is such a famous road. Rising to finish at the glacial Neila lakes, this naughty little ascent has played a pivotal role in deciding the Vuelta a España, and also stars in the annual Vuelta a Burgos. Leaving Quintanar de la Sierra, the first two-thirds are a very gentle affair as the slope ever-so-slightly rises out of the valley. In fact, it's a full 10 kilometres before the proper action starts, and when it does, it comes with a real bang. Upon reaching the Puerto del Collado, the high point of the BU-822, you turn west and the complexion of the climb changes almost instantly. Rising between high conifers, the next four kilometres average close to 10% with ramps as steep as 17%. Constantly changing direction up through the forest, you reach a large clearing and car park with a choice of onward routes: follow the names daubed on the road and take the left fork to climb higher still and into the final push to the lakes. This last part of the climb continues the punishment for a short while, but then fades allowing you to finish somewhat recovered at the beautiful high-altitude lakes.

FACTFILE

DIRECTIONS: Start the climb from the CL-117 heading north through Quintanar de la Sierra on the BU-822.

SUMMIT ALTITUDE	1868m
HEIGHT GAIN	778m
MAXIMUM GRADIENT	17%
AVERAGE GRADIENT	5.3%

MAX GRADIENT **17%**

14.8km

1750m
1500
1250

0   3   6   9   12km

NEILA

BU-822

LAGUNAS DE NEILA

PUERTO DEL COLLADO

QUINTANAR DE LA SIERRA

N-111

CL-117

N-234

SORIA

PALACIOS DE LA SIERRA

CL-117   CL-117

10km

22 Arrate

If the Basque Country is the home of Spanish cycling, then at its heart lies this climb. Seven kilometres with an average gradient just under 7% seems like very little to get excited about, but there is far more to this road than just statistics. Local to two of Spain's most famous bike manufacturers, BH and Orbea, in 1936 it saw the first running of the legendary Subida a Arrate (Climb to Arrate). This soon became one of the most important races in Spain and it was graced by the likes of Luis Ocaña and Federico Bahamontes over the years, the latter winning it five times. Still a key feature of the annual Tour of the Basque Country, the climb starts relatively gently on a 5% slope as you loop over the motorway, before heading north and ramping up. For three kilometres it now averages close to 10% and it's a real grind as there are no hairpins to aim for, just a consistent meander through the forest on the relentlessly hard incline. At roughly the three-kilometre mark, the scenery briefly opens up, then you head back into the trees for more toil before the gentle finale. With six kilometres in the bag, the tough slopes vanish and it's time to stick it in the big ring to smash out the last sector into Arrate while gazing out over the beautiful Basque mountains.

FACTFILE

DIRECTIONS: On the Camino de Arrate in Eibar use the bike lane to reach the junction where you start the climb by taking the GI-3950 towards Arrate.

SUMMIT ALTITUDE	583m
HEIGHT GAIN	449m
MAXIMUM GRADIENT	13%
AVERAGE GRADIENT	6.6%

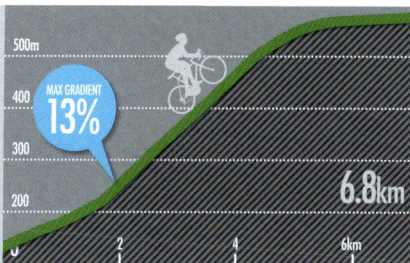

MAX GRADIENT 13%

6.8km

23 Puerto de Urkiola

Another true Basque classic, the climb to the Puerto de Urkiola was once described by local rider Igor Antón as being 'Our Ventoux'. While that's stretching it a bit far – it's nothing like Ventoux geographically – its significance to the region's cyclists is easily on a par. Not long at just shy of six kilometres, but relentlessly hard, you begin the ascent from the village of Mañaria, following the arrows to Urkiola and past the huge ATENCION sign warning of 10% slopes ahead. You'll not find these signs on your average steep road, but as this is the major thoroughfare between Durango and Vitoria-Gasteiz, it is likely to attract traffic that could well struggle on the consistently steep gradient. With the harsh warning burned on to your retinas, you hit the first kilometre which is a relatively steady 8% up through a wonderful snaking S-bend. From here on the slope starts to bite and the 10% gradients begin. At first for just a kilometre before easing back, then almost constant over the last three kilometres to the summit. This really is a climb for your biggest sprocket, one to grind out at walking pace as you revel in the surroundings of the Urkiola Natural Park, before you arrive at the summit at the very welcome brow in the centre of Urkiola.

FACTFILE

DIRECTIONS: Start climbing from the roundabout at the southern point of Mañaria and head south on the BI-623.

SUMMIT ALTITUDE	713m
HEIGHT GAIN	524m
MAXIMUM GRADIENT	12%
AVERAGE GRADIENT	9.2%

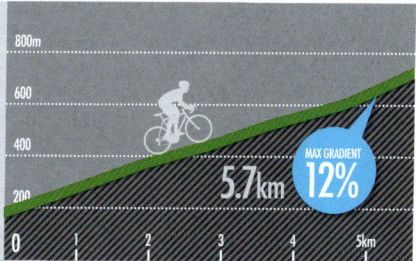

5.7km

MAX GRADIENT 12%

24 Monte Oiz

One of the five Deiadar-Mendiak (Deiadar Mountains) that legend says were once used to send messages across the Basque country, Mount Oiz is home to a simply outrageous collection of roads that make up the three routes to the top. Starting from either Muntibar (the toughest ascent), Gernika or Iurreta (the route I have picked), you are spoilt for choice if you're looking for some quality suffering. Leaving Iurreta, you begin to climb as you leave the roundabout and for the first five kilometres the surface is smooth and the gradient mild. Turning left and following the signs to Monte Oiz, it's all change. The slope kicks up, and the road, no longer asphalt but concrete, narrows to single-car width as it snakes through the forest. For the next five kilometres, you toil across the unforgiving surface in search of the promised grand views ahead. Reaching a solitary building you turn right to next traverse the ridge of the mountain beneath the terrifying whooshing of wind turbine blades. Like giant knives, they slice the sky above your head as you creep up the almost impossibly tough final 1,500 metres. As relentlessly hard as anything I have ridden, the insanity of this finale rewards you with simply gargantuan views across the whole of the Basque Country.

FACTFILE

DIRECTIONS: Start in Iurreta just north of Durango by heading north on Barrio de Goiuria (BI-3341) from the roundabout on Calle de Bidebarrieta (N-634).

SUMMIT ALTITUDE	1020m
HEIGHT GAIN	905m
MAXIMUM GRADIENT	18%
AVERAGE GRADIENT	6%

MAX GRADIENT 18%

15.1km

25 Monte Sollube

There are two sides to this climb: from the south via Larrauri, and from the north, which is the route I have chosen for two reasons. 1: I like the sea views, and 2: I could leave my family in the harbour town of Bermeo to find us somewhere nice for lunch. You can split the ascent into three parts, and the first of these consists of four punishing kilometres of 9% gradient. Once you have found the correct route out of town, the climb starts by heading into a brace of tight bends. Almost immediately you are treated to the wonderful views (if you turn round), and these just get better and better as you rise. Passing through Almike, you weave through the farmland into the shallower gradient of the middle part of the climb which leads you to a junction. Turning right, and then keeping right as the road forks, it's time to begin the final section which starts gently but has a fearsome finish. Up through the forest the sea views are now restricted as you search for the array of radio towers at the top. Creeping up from 7 to 9% the road arrives at a junction. Pause, then turn left to attack the wicked road to the summit. Ahead you are faced with 300 metres of 15% tarmac which kicks up through an even steeper hairpin to finish at the very top of this famous Basque mountain.

FACTFILE

DIRECTIONS: Start from the junction of Camino de Ander Deuna, Carretera de Almike and Carretera de Artike by taking the middle route south to Almike.

SUMMIT ALTITUDE	681m
HEIGHT GAIN	676m
MAXIMUM GRADIENT	15%
AVERAGE GRADIENT	8%

MAX GRADIENT **15%**

8.5km

BERMEO • BAY OF BISCAY
MUNGIA
BILBAO GERNIKA MUTRIKU
BI-633 AP-8
A-8 EIBAR
DURANGO
AP-68 N-240 N-636 BERGARA
AP-1

BAKIO **BERMEO**
MUNDAKA
BI-2101
BI-631
BI-2235

I arrived at climb number one on my final research trip, following the 1,097-mile drive from Sheffield, to be faced with an absolute wall. A signature ascent on the annual Vuelta a Burgos, the Picón Blanco has two ways to the summit, but it's the route out of Espinosa de los Monteros which you must ride. Turning off the Calle del Sol you will spot the bright orange signs that will direct you out of town and on to the gentle early slopes. I say gentle, they actually average around 8%, but trust me, in the context of this climb, that's gentle. After roughly three kilometres, in a small patch of conifers, you'll pass a wonderfully informative and detailed sign that paints quite a daunting picture of what lies ahead. I'm sure the local authorities had good intentions, but one glance at the last five kilometres where the route profile turns from red to black is enough to make you want to stop and turn back. From here on in, it's proper tough. With only a handful of bends towards the summit to break the grind, and little or no shelter from any trees to shield you from the infamous winds that swirl around this peak, you face a real battle. Heading straight on at a split in the road, the finish sits amongst the crumbling concrete of the abandoned military base, covered in graffiti and populated by wild horses – a suitably brutalist backdrop to a thoroughly brutal climb.

FACTFILE

DIRECTIONS: Leave the Calle del Sol (BU-570) that runs through the centre of Espinosa de los Monteros to start the climb by turning east on Calle del Montero.

SUMMIT ALTITUDE	1519m
HEIGHT GAIN	768m
MAXIMUM GRADIENT	15%
AVERAGE GRADIENT	9.3%

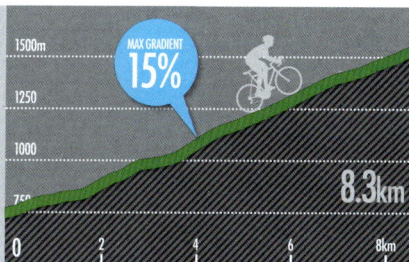

MAX GRADIENT **15%**

8.3km

LOS TORNOS ★

A-8 LAREDO
COLINDRES A-8 ALGORTA

BILBAO

N-629 GÜENES
LLODIO

ESPINOSA DE LOS MONTEROS

N-629

BERCEDO

N-629

27 Puerto de Orduña

Starting in the Basque Country and rising to cross the border into Castile and León, the climb to the Puerto de Orduña is a near-perfect mountain test. Heading south towards the imposing ridge, this road once dubbed 'the engine breaker' is thankfully not quite as fearsome as that name might imply. With an average slope of 7.6%, there really is nothing along its path that will prove that uncomfortable. Heading directly south from Orduña, the ascent begins after passing under a railway bridge then starts to sway gently right to left. As you hit the base of the mountain wall that blocks your way, these gentle meanders morph into a flurry of fabulous hairpins – seven tightly packed bends that swish you back and forth. Although, as they're all hidden in the trees, you'll only get the odd glimpse of the ever-evolving view. Smooth, wide and potentially busy at times on account of it being a prominent route, the climb eventually exits the forest to reveal the whole of northern Spain on your left and the towering bare rock face on your right. Now hugging the edge of the mountain, you've two more sets of twin hairpins to negotiate before the toughest climbing ends and the gentle stroll to the summit begins. Take a good look as you turn your back on the incredible vista, then push on, and even though you may think you have finished, don't sit up until you pass the summit sign.

FACTFILE

DIRECTIONS: Head south from Orduña on the A-625, then after the last roundabout pass under the railway bridge and start the climb.

SUMMIT ALTITUDE	900m
HEIGHT GAIN	592m
MAXIMUM GRADIENT	11%
AVERAGE GRADIENT	7.6%

MAX GRADIENT **11%** **7.8km**

28 Puerto de Alisas

Heading south into the Cantabrian Mountains, this climb is a gateway to adventure, an escape route from the coast into the jagged interior. In my opinion this is the better side, but it's also a decent climb ridden the other way, heading north from Arredondo. The first four kilometres are very steady, allowing your legs to warm up, then gradually the gradient starts to increase until it assumes the consistent 6–7% slope that takes you all the way to the top. With a modest summit height of just 674 metres, the majority of the climb is wooded and it's not until you reach the first hairpin that the views arrive. When they do, they are well worth the wait, and the final three and a half kilometres through eight switchbacks on the steady 7% slope are a real treat. Never presenting any real difficulty, you'll swing through the corners, and the village of Las Calzadillas, as you drink in the mountain vistas that stretch to the ocean below. Romping towards the summit, you'll feel like Alberto Contador as you finish the climb at pace, passing the two car parks before rolling down the other side in search of the next, maybe more challenging, ascent.

FACTFILE

DIRECTIONS: From the centre of La Cavada, climb south-east on the CA-261, the Avenida de Alisas, away from the bridge over the Río Miera.

SUMMIT ALTITUDE	674m
HEIGHT GAIN	614m
MAXIMUM GRADIENT	8%
AVERAGE GRADIENT	4.8%

MAX GRADIENT **8%**

12.7km

600m / 400 / 200 / 0 / 3 / 6 / 9 / 12km

SANTANDER — NOJA — COLINDRES — VALDECILLA — LA CAVADA — TORRELAVEGA — S-30 — A-8 — CA-643 — CA-262 — CA-261 — CA-265 — N-623 — A-67 — 10km

LA CAVADA — LIÉRGANES — BARRIO DE ARRIBA — CA-260 — ALTO DE LOS ESCAJOS — CA-261

29 Alto de los Machucos

I'd seen this climb on TV, I'd listened to the hysterics from the commentators as they waxed lyrical about its savage 28% gradient, and I believed I'd done sufficient research into what lay ahead, but oh how wrong I was. Leaving Bustablado, deep in the valley, there is a sense of foreboding in the air as you tackle a nasty ramp out of the village, but this isn't the climb, not just yet. Los Machucos starts after you turn left, plummet down to cross a river and then face the road rearing up the other side. From here, it is a torture chamber. Each of the early vicious ramps takes its toll, and then you reach the big one, a gargantuan stretch of simply ludicrous 20–30% gradient. Once through a slight midway hiatus, you appear to be riding into a cul-de-sac of towering rock with no obvious way through. It looks impossible for a road to escape this rock fortress, but Los Machucos somehow does. Entering the woods, it is time for the famed concrete switchbacks: 20%, 25%, maybe even steeper, but by now you really will be beyond caring. With the showpiece corners conquered, there's still more, and leaving the woods you dare not look up. You have to keep going though, higher and higher until the summit eventually arrives at a sharp right-hand bend. UTTERLY HIDEOUS.

FACTFILE

DIRECTIONS: Leave the CA-261 and ride into Bustablado. Head through and out the other side of the village, take the first left, drop down and then up.

SUMMIT ALTITUDE	921m
HEIGHT GAIN	618m
MAXIMUM GRADIENT	28%
AVERAGE GRADIENT	10.5%

MAX GRADIENT 28%

5.9km

A long climb that can be split into two distinct acts, both of which feature a stunning and dramatic finale. Act one kicks off from the Cantabrian town of Arredondo on the banks of the river Asón. Travelling south, the first four kilometres are very shallow as around you the valley sides begin to rise. Before long, the slope starts to creep up to settle into a solid 7% pitch as it heads towards the vertical wall of rock ahead, and it soon becomes apparent that it's going to have to do something pretty spectacular to escape the valley. Ditching its direct north–south direction, the road now scales the limestone wall ahead via a series of four giant switchbacks which open up monumental views back down the valley. The narrow path cuts its way through the jagged landscape, heading skywards to peak at the Puerto del Asón where drinks can be taken during a slight interval in climbing. Over this peak you drop to a junction to take the right fork and begin act two. Through much more open scenery and with vast views opening out on your left, you get stuck into more 7% slopes on the remaining eight kilometres to the top. The finish of the second act comes, via one last hairpin, at the cleft in the road alongside the grand stone summit marker and the border with Castile and León.

FACTFILE

DIRECTIONS: Leave Arredondo and start climbing on Barrio del Bao by turning off the CA-261 on to the CA-265 towards Asón.

SUMMIT ALTITUDE	1200m
HEIGHT GAIN	1114m
MAXIMUM GRADIENT	10%
AVERAGE GRADIENT	5.4%

MAX GRADIENT
10%

20.5km

Not that this climb doesn't merit a place in the book by rights, but it actually came off the bench to replace the Picón del Fraile after I was turned away at the top there by men with guns. The longest ascent travels north to south and its origins can be traced back to the town of Liérganes just off the A-8 motorway. The first kilometres out of the town are nothing to worry about, and it spends a long time following the Río Miera up the valley to start climbing properly once you have crossed a narrow bridge. Now on the east bank of the river, the roads rises for three kilometres on a slope that reaches 10% in places. Be ready, as after this initial sharp rise there is a short descent where you can shake out your legs before settling into the long pull to the top. Passing numerous small villages and sheltered by long patches of forest and towering cliffs, you grind your way to the stunning climax. Passing La Concha, the complexion of the road changes wholesale – now it's exposed and open. From here to the top the narrow road – as if slashed out of the empty hillside by a giant rapier – passes through a series of giant zigzags on a 6–7% slope to arrive at the summit and the border with Castile and León.

FACTFILE

DIRECTIONS: Travelling south from Liérganes, this climb kicks off in earnest at the bridge where the CA-643 crosses from the west to the east side of the Río Miera.

SUMMIT ALTITUDE	1338m
HEIGHT GAIN	1138m
MAXIMUM GRADIENT	10%
AVERAGE GRADIENT	5.1%

MAX GRADIENT **10%**

22.3km

32 Peña Cabarga

An archetypal Vuelta a España summit finish, Peña Cabarga is a 20% dead-end road which has hosted four stage finishes (so far), two of which were taken by Chris Froome (in 2011 and 2016). Froome's first victory, the moment he really announced himself on the world stage, is immortalised in one of the best cycling clips you will find on YouTube as he battles Juan José Cobo at astronomical speeds on the wicked slopes. Its proximity to Santander guarantees it is smothered in fans come race day, but hopefully when you arrive it will be nice and quiet as heading south the gradient wastes no time getting stuck into your legs, with the first kilometre set on a 10% average. Bending left, next comes the relatively gentle middle section as you rise through the Parque de la Naturaleza de Cabárceno, hugging the edge of the conical hill. Once round the other side of the mound, the slope really begins to bite as you start the savage final two kilometres. Cutting across the rocky landscape, in and out of hairpins, the pitch kicks up to 16% as it searches for the summit. Into the last kilometre, free from any tree coverage and with uninterrupted views, it just gets harder and harder all the way to the peak which is adorned with monumental radio masts.

FACTFILE

DIRECTIONS: Start by heading south from the Carretera de Nacional Santander following the signs to Santiago de Cudeyo and Peña Cabarga.

SUMMIT ALTITUDE	562m
HEIGHT GAIN	536m
MAXIMUM GRADIENT	18%
AVERAGE GRADIENT	9.4%

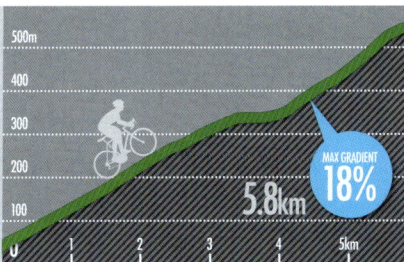

MAX GRADIENT 18%

5.8km

This is exactly why we all ride bikes: to be able to ride a 20-kilometre climb on a sublime mountain road through pristine scenery. Leaving Espinilla, the ascent heads due west to puncture the wilderness, a solitary road surrounded on all sides by rocky peaks. The slope is gentle into La Lomba, then out the other side it starts to kick up a little more as hugging a perfect 6% slope it begins to make its way out of the vast valley. With hardly any obstruction to your views, you are exposed to the elements the entire way up, so this is not a climb for a wet day! At kilometre 16 you reach Brañavieja and then the ski village of Alto Campoo, the gateway to the climb's glorious finale. Approaching the border with Castile and León, and passing the ski infrastructure that somewhat blights the landscape, you head towards the horizon. For the most part the gradient has been pretty relaxed, but now it bites as you scale the mountainside to the summit. Peaking at 16%, this last push through the barren land on a marvellously smooth road delivers you to an insanely magnificent viewpoint. Sitting right on the ridge of the mountain and offering views of equal wonder on both sides, it's a place that on a clear day is very hard to leave.

FACTFILE

DIRECTIONS: Start from the roundabout in the centre of Espinilla and head west on to the end of the CA-183 following the sign to Alto Campoo.

SUMMIT ALTITUDE	1987m
HEIGHT GAIN	1057m
MAXIMUM GRADIENT	16%
AVERAGE GRADIENT	4.9%

MAX GRADIENT **16%**

21.3km

My morning on this climb is one I'll never forget as under blanket skies I wound my way to its secluded base beneath the towering rock pinnacles that line the Río Cares. Passing the few buildings that make up the settlement of Poncebos, the atmosphere was deathly quiet, then once across the river I set upon the transition from dark valley to rise into the light. The slope is immediately hard, with three solid kilometres of 8–10% average, and still trapped between gargantuan towers of jagged rock you toil upwards. Following this severe beginning, the climb cuts you some slack and retires to a more modest 6% for a while as it passes the village of Tielve, still framed on both sides by near-vertical rock faces. Continuing on to Sotres, the scenery is utterly immense – it's just pure savage beauty. Beneath your wheels, you'll feel the gradient begin to bite more as well, as it starts to tip up and up on the approach to the mountaintop village. With two kilometres of double-digit average and ramps of 20%, this section is the hardest of the whole ascent, and twisting through Sotres it delivers you to an intermediate summit at the Collado de Caballar. Here, the brutal incline ends and for the remaining journey to the eventual lonely and remote summit, the ride is far easier.

FACTFILE

DIRECTIONS: Ride south on the AS-264 away from the AS-114 through the valley to Poncebos. Start the climb after crossing the bridge and passing the car park.

SUMMIT ALTITUDE	1317m
HEIGHT GAIN	1099m
MAXIMUM GRADIENT	20%
AVERAGE GRADIENT	7.5%

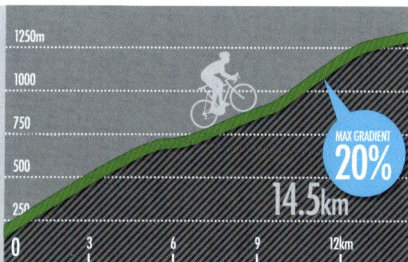

MAX GRADIENT **20%**

14.5km

35 Lagos de Covadonga

Arguably the most famous climb in Spain and certainly the most significant in modern Vuelta history, the road to the Lagos de Covadonga rises into the Picos de Europa where it ends at the glacial lakes in the centre of the national park. First included in the 1983 race, it has featured over 20 times since, therefore cementing its relationship with the Grand Tour forever. Heading south, the approach to the climb winds along the valley floor and although a modicum of elevation is gained the real action doesn't kick in until you reach the second roundabout in Covadonga. Rising off to the left, the increase in gradient is dramatic as immediately you're fighting a 10% average that lasts for almost four kilometres. First rising through thick woodland, the curvaceous road relentlessly pounds your legs, then once free of tree cover its true magnificence is revealed. Now in immaculate open scenery, this next sector goes by the name La Huescra and boasts almost 800 metres of near-15% slope. Following this brutality, the next part of the climb is a touch easier as it weaves through the primordial landscape surrounded by sensational views. With 14.5 kilometres covered, there's a small descent then just the final ramp; one last kilometre of hurt to finally reach the lakes.

FACTFILE

DIRECTIONS: Head south from the AS-114, following the signs to La Riera and Covadonga, then start the climb from the second roundabout in Covadonga.

SUMMIT ALTITUDE	1120m
HEIGHT GAIN	830m
MAXIMUM GRADIENT	15%
AVERAGE GRADIENT	7.5%

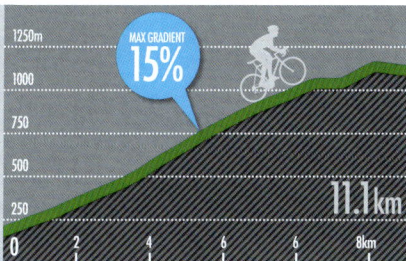

MAX GRADIENT
15%

11.1km

COLUNGA
A-8
LLANES
CANGAS DE ONIS
AS-114
N-625

AS-114
CORAO
CANGAS DE ONIS
SOTO DE CANGAS
MESTAS DE CON
AS-114
LA RIERA
N-625
COVADONGA
PARQUE NACIONAL PICOS DE EUROPA
N-625

36 Collado de Llesba

The majority of this climb belongs to the Puerto de San Glorio which links Cantabria with Castile and León and which I have chosen to ride the more favoured way, east to west from Potes. Sticking to the N-621 for nearly 27 kilometres, this is a long climb but one that's never too steep. In fact, the first six kilometres hardly rise at all, but then once past the town of La Vega you will feel gravity start to pull. Settling into a steady 6–7% slope, you can pretty much pick a gear and ride that all the way to the top providing your legs hold out. Passing the villages of Bores and Enterrias, the road then crosses into the southern reaches of the Picos de Europa National Park for its final hairpin-filled kilometres. Surrounded by lush green peaks, the Puerto de San Glorio weaves towards its summit which arrives at a modest plateau where, instead of rolling down the other side, it's time to take on the short two-kilometre appendage up to the Collado de Llesba. Turning right, the road narrows and there's a short concrete section before it continues on roughly sealed asphalt. Now, you might be expecting two kilometres of vicious 20% slope here, but alas I have to disappoint; I'm afraid it's just more shallow gradient with a spellbinding view out in front of you all the way to the very top. Never mind.

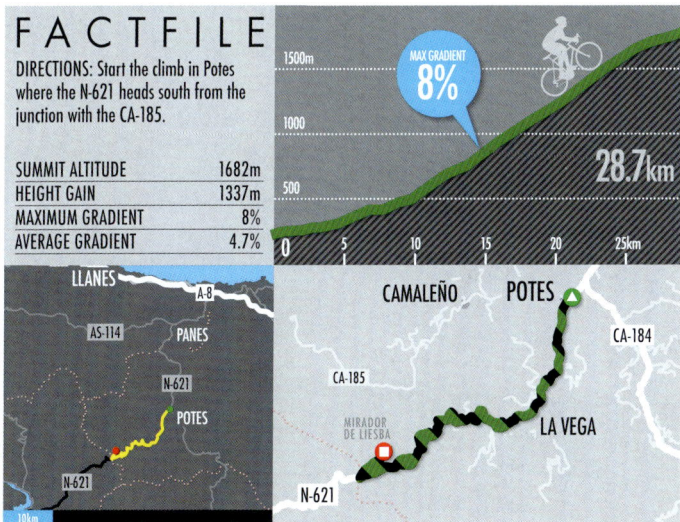

FACTFILE

DIRECTIONS: Start the climb in Potes where the N-621 heads south from the junction with the CA-185.

SUMMIT ALTITUDE	1682m
HEIGHT GAIN	1337m
MAXIMUM GRADIENT	8%
AVERAGE GRADIENT	4.7%

MAX GRADIENT
8%

28.7km

LLANES
A-8
AS-114
PANES
N-621
POTES
N-621
10km

CAMALEÑO
POTES
CA-185
CA-184
MIRADOR DE LLESBA
LA VEGA
N-621

37 Alto de La Camperona

Unfortunately, this is one climb I never got to ride. I know, I'm a fraud, I'm sorry. Visiting in 2014 when the Vuelta was using it for a summit finish, it was just too busy to ride by the time we arrived, so we were forced to walk up, which if it's any consolation was still bloody hard. Watching the race that day, the leaders danced up it oblivious, but those not built for climbing were in some real trouble, with more than one rider almost coming to a complete halt in front of us. Leaving Sotillos, this brutal road heads north in search of its summit on a narrow path with no signs at the bottom to guide you. Averaging 12.4% with ramps far steeper makes its three kilometres seem like 30. As soon as it starts to weave around, the slope kicks up and you will click down as you head round a couple of tight bends. Through these and you are into the mid-section of the climb which is where the real suffering is to be found. Broken into three parts between three bends, there's almost two kilometres of close to 20% average. It is now just a case of survival as you crawl on up to the oh-so-welcome finish which lies on a knife-edge at the very top of the small mountain.

FACTFILE

DIRECTIONS: To the west of the small church in Sotillos, take the second road north. It's not marked but you will know it's the right one when it starts to hurt.

SUMMIT ALTITUDE	1597m
HEIGHT GAIN	369m
MAXIMUM GRADIENT	25%
AVERAGE GRADIENT	12.4%

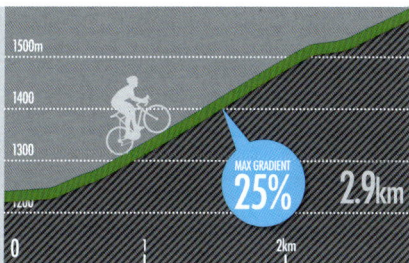

I first rode this beast in the autumn of 2014. Full of bravado, I hit its slopes armed with a 39 at the front and a 28 at the back and it duly pulled my pants down and spanked me. Never before had I been beaten by a mountain and had to do the walk of shame, but never before had I come up against a foe as mighty as the Angliru. Leaving La Vega, the first few kilometres are relatively tame, and they are followed by a short levelling and descent. Following this, however, the madness begins. Hitting you in waves, the sections of stupid-steep 20%+ gradient suck the very marrow out of your bones. One of these savage stretches of gradient you could cope with, it's just all of them added together that keeps punching you until you can't take any more. Each vicious section has a name, such as Les Picones, Cobayos or El Aviru, and, the worst of the lot, Cueña les Cabres. With three kilometres to go, it's here that I was forced to dismount; it was either walk or snap my knees. Reaching 24% at its peak but spending far too long above 20%, this is where the Angliru seals its reputation. Following on, there are more hard ramps, but shorter so allowing better recovery, and then the final kilometre is all but flat to allow you to compose yourself and arrive triumphant at the summit.

FACTFILE

DIRECTIONS: In the centre of La Vega, leave the AS-231 and head west on the RI-2 down the small descent following the sign to Cima L'Angliru.

SUMMIT ALTITUDE	1570m
HEIGHT GAIN	1248m
MAXIMUM GRADIENT	24%
AVERAGE GRADIENT	9.9%

MAX GRADIENT **24%**

1500m
1250m
1000m
750m
500m

12.5km

3   6   9   12km

A-63   OVIEDO   A-66   AS-1
A-63   A-64
AS-229   AS-231
POLA DE LENA
AP-66
10km

LA FOZ
AS-231
L'ARA
LA VEGA
AS-231

39 Alto del Gamoniteiro

First on everyone's list for riding in Asturias is naturally the Angliru, as that's the really famous climb. But what if I was to tell you that there is an even better ascent just a few miles south? Sharing what is essentially the same mountain, the road to Alto del Gamoniteiro may not be quite as tough as the Angliru, but it's totally mind-blowing and I'd say one of the three most beautiful climbs I have ever ridden. There are two ways to start: either heading east on the AS-230 from Bárzana, or – the best way – riding west from Pola de Lena. The first part is essentially the climb to the Alto de la Cobertoria on an immaculate winding road which pretty much climbs at a constant 10% for almost 9 kilometres. OUCH. Before you reach the summit of La Cobertoria though, you take the right turn off the main carriageway and into the primitive landscape that covers this mountain. The road, now a sliver of tarmac, often rough and periodically broken, creeps across the rocky scenery in search of its summit. Starting on a 10% gradient and never relenting, it becomes incrementally harder as it climbs. Faced with prolonged bursts of 15 and even 17% gradient towards the top, progress is slow, but such are your surroundings you could ride this road for eternity.

FACTFILE

DIRECTIONS: Leave Calle de Vital Aza in Pola de Lena and start the climb on the AS-230 following the sign to Bárzana.

SUMMIT ALTITUDE	1770m
HEIGHT GAIN	1462m
MAXIMUM GRADIENT	17%
AVERAGE GRADIENT	8.9%

MAX GRADIENT **17%**

16.4km

40 Puerto de la Cubilla

La Cubilla is known affectionately as the Asturian Galibier, in reference to its uncharacteristically long length for the region and because it's an equally stunning road. It didn't make its Vuelta debut until 2019, which is unbelievable when you see the scenery it traverses. Heading south from Campomanes, the first 11 kilometres are really steady through the villages of Sotiello and Espinedo, then, when it reaches Telledo, the slope kicks up a little more. As a few hairpins arrive you're soon faced with some 10% gradient, but this harsh interlude is only brief and before long the pitch returns to a moderate 5–6%. From Telledo and for the next 13 kilometres the road ambles westwards through intermittent woodland, around the odd hairpin and past lonely farmhouses. Then, after rounding a tight right-hand bend that's wrapped around the edge of an outcrop of rock, the surroundings change. You are now transported into the high mountains as the road snakes across the barren slopes surrounded by exposed peaks. Still never climbing beyond 7%, there are no horrors in store on this road, just pure secluded beauty. The final stretch eases to a 3% slope and presents you with an armchair view out east over the mountains as you close in on the summit.

FACTFILE

DIRECTIONS: Start from the crossroads in the middle of Campomanes and follow the LN-8 out the back of town and under the AP-66 motorway.

SUMMIT ALTITUDE	1683m
HEIGHT GAIN	1293m
MAXIMUM GRADIENT	11%
AVERAGE GRADIENT	4.6%

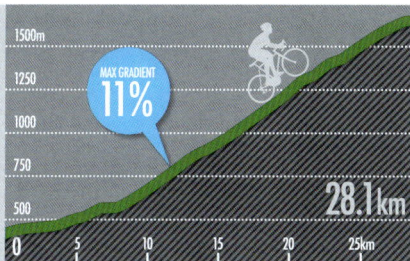

MAX GRADIENT
11%

28.1km

1500m
1250
1000
750
500

0   5   10   15   20   25km

CAMPOMANES

SOTIELLO

TELLEDO

AP-66

N-630

PARQUE NATURAL
DE LAS UBIÑAS-LA
MESA

AS-228

LE-481

PUERTO
DE PAJARES

AS-227

AS-229

LA RIERA

POLA
DE LENA

CAMPOMANES

VILLABLINO

AP-66

N-630

10km

41 Cuitu Negru

The Puerto de Pajares, which forms the first part of this climb, has long been of major importance to this region, linking Oviedo with Léon way before the Vuelta arrived in 1945. Nowadays, the AP-66 is the primary artery between the two cities, however this climb does still attract more than its fair share of traffic, so be warned, it can be uncomfortably busy. For the first seven kilometres the gradient is very shallow, little more than a false flat, then in the mid-section it begins to increase, briefly to around the 8% mark then falling back again for a few kilometres at 5%. It's only the end of the pass that really carries any bite as the slope gradually increases until you hit the killer finish, a really nasty ramp that peaks at 17% shortly before the top. Once past the cafés that mark the Puerto and to really punish your legs, roll along a few hundred metres then take the right turn to head for Cuitu Negru. This now-classic Vuelta finish was first used in the 2012 race and features gradients in excess of 24% on its way to the high-altitude ski station. Riding through Brañillin, take the very narrow road out past the Cafetería Telesilla to start 2.5 kilometres of brutality. First climbing at around 15%, then 12%, it ends at the top of the world with a full kilometre at over 20%. SAVAGE.

FACTFILE

DIRECTIONS: Simply ride out of Campomanes on the N-630 and start to climb.

SUMMIT ALTITUDE	1838m
HEIGHT GAIN	1454m
MAXIMUM GRADIENT	24%
AVERAGE GRADIENT	5.6%

MAX GRADIENT 24%

25.8km

1500m
1000m
500m

0   5   10   15   20   25km

AS-227
AS-229
LA RIERA
POLA DE LENA
CAMPOMANES
VILLABLINO
AP-66   N-630

10km

CAMPOMANES
SOTIELLO
PARQUE NATURAL DE LAS UBIÑAS-LA MESA
AP-66
PUERTO DE PAJARES
N-630

42 Ermita de Alba

Fitting the current blueprint of a modern Vuelta climb exactly (basically an old goat track that has been covered in asphalt), the Ermita de Alba was brought to the attention of the global cycling community during the 2015 race. Looking at the raw statistics – 6.6 kilometres at an average of 11 3% – it doesn't sound too bad, but believe me, it's far worse. Turning east off the AS-230 and following the sign to the Capilla de Alba, immediately you start to climb. Although not as long as the neighbouring Angliru, this road is certainly as steep with multiple ramps well beyond 20%. Twisting through meadows lined with an old wooden fence, there is something almost Swiss about the surroundings as you grind pedal rev by pedal rev upwards. Passing the villages of Salcedo and Las Villinas, you have finished the 'easy' part of the climb and next comes the real fun. With the last four individual kilometres averaging 12, 11.5, 11 and 16%, and with much steeper stretches within them, you can see why the Vuelta organisers knew they had found a real gem. Saving the best until last, the final horrendous 300 metres to the eventual summit at times reach the magical 30%, ensuring that like me you'll collapse over your handlebars when you can climb no further.

FACTFILE

DIRECTIONS: From the AS-230, just north of Bárzana, head east up the ramp following the signs to Salcedo and the Capilla de Alba.

SUMMIT ALTITUDE	1190m
HEIGHT GAIN	746m
MAXIMUM GRADIENT	30%
AVERAGE GRADIENT	11.3%

MAX GRADIENT 30%

6.6km

43 Alto de la Farrapona

A new favourite Vuelta summit finish and a popular tourist destination, this climb rises into the pristine beauty of the Somiedo Natural Park. One of the most unspoiled wildernesses left in Spain, these mountains are home to vultures, golden eagles, wolves and even bears. The climb begins as you leave the AS-227 across a small bridge and directly into a tunnel following the signs to Saliencia. Emerging from the dark, you enter a magical natural world, the road trapped on both sides by towering walls of rock. The first 13 kilometres of the climb will do nothing to hurt your legs, apart from perhaps a slightly tougher section at around the seven-kilometre mark. The final six kilometres, however, are a different story. All averaging close to 9% and with a multitude of ramps hitting 12%, they make for an arduous finale. Having barely diverted from its path up through the valley, with two kilometres to go it begins to squirm and you're treated to a flurry of hairpins between the jagged rocks before the summit arrives at the car park for the Lagos de Saliencia. Here the tarmac abruptly ends and, turning to gravel, the road disappears into the wilderness over the other side. Oh, and so long as you don't mind pushing your bike a bit, the lakes are definitely worth the trek to visit.

FACTFILE

DIRECTIONS: Leave the AS-227 at the junction with the Carretera de Saliencia, heading due east across the small bridge and through the tunnel.

SUMMIT ALTITUDE	1708m
HEIGHT GAIN	1079m
MAXIMUM GRADIENT	15%
AVERAGE GRADIENT	5.8%

MAX GRADIENT
15%

18.7km

8/10

PUERTO DE
ANCARES

Cima: 4 Km
P. media a
cima: 6,2 %
Altitud: 1.410 m

44 Puerto de Ancares

Of the four ways to the summit of the Puerto de Ancares, two leave Murias de Rao heading south, one rises eastwards from Donís and the last heads north from Tejedo de Ancares. They are all packed with tough gradient with many kilometres above 10%, and arguably the hardest is the route from Tejedo, but I have chosen to include the climb from Murias through Pan do Zarco. It takes some effort to find the base hidden in the Serra dos Ancares mountains, and it starts with a jumble of hairpins. Navigating around Murias you come to a crossroads: heading left leads to the village, and heading right, turning back on yourself, leads to the mountains. What follows are six insane kilometres of over 10% slope (and in places steeper) on a road that's little more than a gravel farm track. Narrow, quiet, rough and rugged, and with nothing in the way of corners, it grinds on and up towards the wall of peaks that lines the horizon. After passing the tiny settlement of Pan do Zarco, the slope recedes slightly, but you still have the loose surface to contend with all the way to join the main road. From the junction where three routes converge, head straight over to tackle one last giant hairpin, which boasts the most stupendous views, and then the final 16% ramp to the finish.

FACTFILE

DIRECTIONS: The base lies in the gully just below the village of Murias de Rao on the LU-P-3508 as it crosses the Rio Balouta.

SUMMIT ALTITUDE	1670m
HEIGHT GAIN	1112m
MAXIMUM GRADIENT	16%
AVERAGE GRADIENT	9.5%

MAX GRADIENT 16%

11.7km

VILLABLINO
LE-4211
CL-631
TORENO
LE-711
BEMBIBRE
A-6
A-6
N-120
PONFERRADA

ROBLEDO DE RAO   AS-212
PARQUE NATURAL DE LAS FUENTES DEL NARCEA, DEGAÑA E IBIAS
MURIAS DE RAO
BALOUTA
SUARBOL
LE-4211

45 Peña de la Escurpia

I rode this climb at first light one warm August morning, leaving the family sleeping in the hotel room. Starting the ascent, I was the only person I could see anywhere, but then as I climbed, I started to spot walkers tramping through the bushes either side. Then more and more, all loaded up with packs. What was going on? It transpires that this climb lies on the route of the world-famous Camino de Santiago pilgrim trail which converges at the Santiago de Compostela cathedral in Galicia. So, if there's a bustle in the hedgerow, don't be alarmed, it's just a pilgrim! To the climb, riding against the flow of 'traffic', it rises up from Molinaseca averaging a very gentle 6% all the way through the village of Riego de Ambrós and into El Acebo. This second settlement seems to be a popular watering hole for weary travellers and is beautiful to ride through with its smooth cobbled streets. Through El Acebo and the gradient now begins to hurt a little with a few sections of 10 and 11% as it weaves through a sequence of tight bends. With two kilometres to go, there's a slight dip, followed by an easy stretch which leads to the toughest 500 metres of the climb, ensuring you have to work on your quest, albeit against the flow, to find the summit of this wonderful road.

FACTFILE

DIRECTIONS: Start the climb after crossing the Río Meruelo and heading south out of Molinaseca on Travesía Manuel Fraga, the LE-142.

SUMMIT ALTITUDE	1494m
HEIGHT GAIN	908m
MAXIMUM GRADIENT	15%
AVERAGE GRADIENT	6.5%

MAX GRADIENT **15%**

14km

CATALUÑA

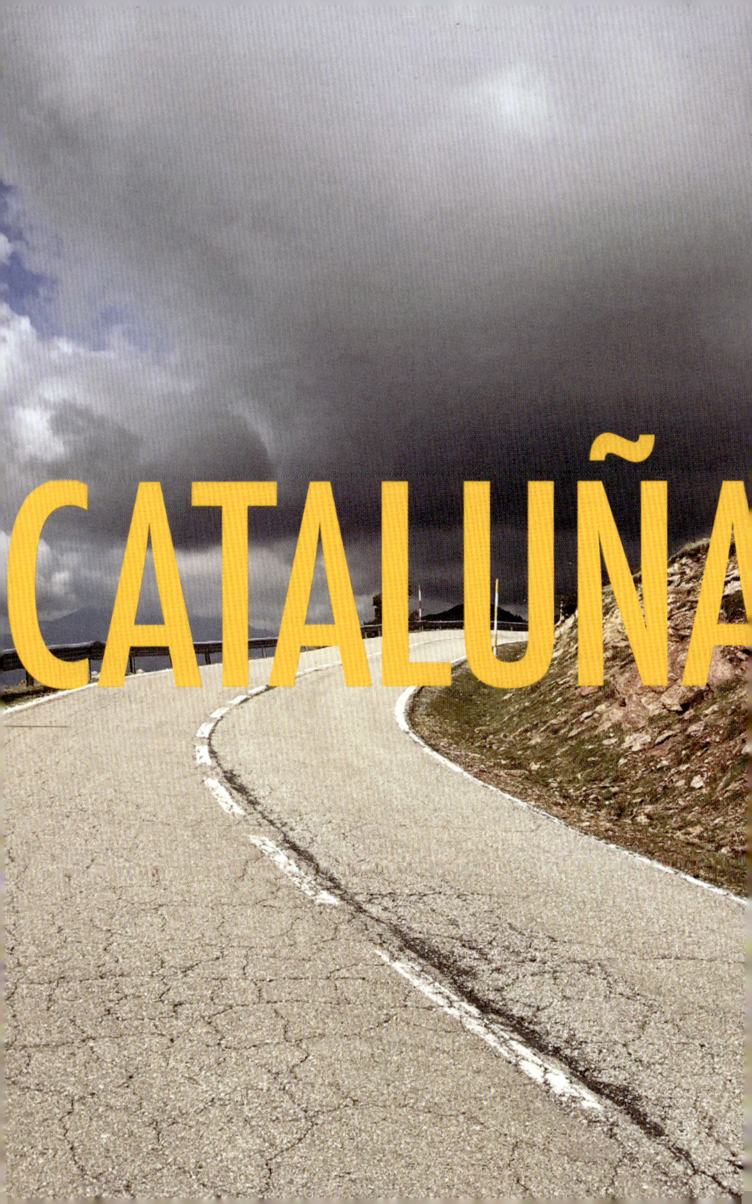

46 Mare de Déu dels Àngels

If every climb was as hard as say the Angliru (page 95), then I wager cycling up mountains wouldn't be quite such a popular pastime. In fact, there would probably be just a hard core of a few hundred masochists out there beating themselves up on stupid gradients each weekend with everyone else sticking to the flat. Thankfully, every mountain road isn't a savage beast, and many – like this one – are simply divine. Its proximity to Girona, twinned with its mild-mannered slope, make Els Àngels a very popular destination, and straight off the plane it was the perfect road to get my legs turning after a long day of travelling. At 10 kilometres long it's not short, but with an average slope of just 3.5% it's about as easy a challenge as you'll find. Heading east from Girona, the climbing comes in two sections, the first lasting about four kilometres followed by a plateau and small descent, then the last four kilometres ramping up to the summit. Smooth, wide and sheltered by trees, the road curves gently through the forest, not once raising a fist in anger. When you reach the apex and before you drop down the other side, be sure to finish the job by turning left to complete the final 200 metres to the Els Àngels sanctuary from where you can take in the views over the Catalan hills.

FACTFILE

DIRECTIONS: Head east from Girona on the GIV-6703, pass under the N-11 and start to climb.

SUMMIT ALTITUDE	470m
HEIGHT GAIN	359m
MAXIMUM GRADIENT	8%
AVERAGE GRADIENT	3.6%

MAX GRADIENT **8%**

10.1km

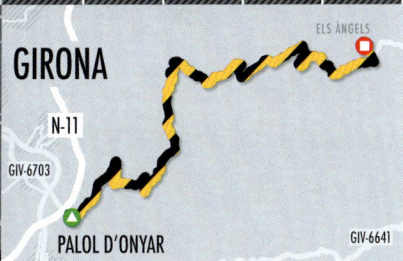

If you head east out of Girona up Els Àngels, maybe for a short loop or to explore the wonderful coastline, then there's no better way back into the city than via this climb to the Santa Pellaia church. Like Els Àngels, it's another steady, toothless ascent – nothing to hurt you, nothing to scare you, just six lovely kilometres of gentle gradient. Heading west from La Bisbal d'Empordà on the GI-664, you pass through Cruïlles, then Sant Sadurní de l'Heura, to start the climb at the point where the road turns sharp left across a small bridge. From here to the top the ascent is a hectic combination of turns; not *lacets* carved into the hillside, but a barrage of deviations in direction through the forested hills. With the toughest slopes at the bottom, a mere 1,500 metres of 6%, the pitch then dips to hover around the 3–4% mark from there on in. If you were new to cycling up mountains and had to pick somewhere to start, then I'd say this is the ideal spot; then just keep searching for harder and harder climbs as you get fitter. The summit arrives at a 90-degree bend in the road where a small track takes you down to the church, or continue on to descend via Cassà de la Selva back to Girona.

FACTFILE

DIRECTIONS: Head west from Sant Sadurní de l'Heura on the GI-664 and start the climb around 5 kilometres later after passing over the small bridge.

SUMMIT ALTITUDE	361 m
HEIGHT GAIN	241 m
MAXIMUM GRADIENT	6%
AVERAGE GRADIENT	4.1%

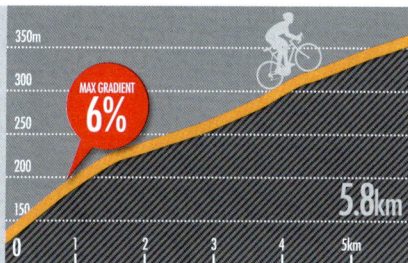

MAX GRADIENT
6%

5.8km

48 Rocacorba

Girona has been a hotbed of cycling for years now, a favoured base for expat pros and consequently very popular with the cycling fashionista. Offering the perfect hub for all types of riding, together with a kind climate and excellent transport links, the region's signature climb is the Rocacorba. It's not a pretty road, in fact it's possibly the most overhyped climb in Spain, but one look at the leaderboard on Strava and you'll see all the big hitters have been out to put down a time. If it wasn't for this connection with pro cycling, it wouldn't merit a place in this book, but the notoriety it has gained from riders pushing themselves to the edge up its demanding slopes justifies its inclusion. The base lies close to Banyoles (much quieter than Girona if you are planning a visit), following a couple of kilometres of riding across the flat valley floor. Only given a coat of tarmac in 2000, the testing 10-kilometre ascent starts as you cross a small bridge – and then you got for it. The pros all aim to get under 30 minutes, fit amateurs under 50 minutes, and there is little or nothing to distract you from your task as almost the entire climb is shrouded in thick forest. There are a few hairpins to aim for, and the odd building, but it's all about the effort as you search for the summit, which sitting beneath a jumble of telecoms towers does finally reward you with a pretty decent view.

FACTFILE

DIRECTIONS: Head west out of Banyoles on the GI-524 then take the turn south on to the GIV-5247 towards Pujarnol. Start the climb after crossing the small river.

SUMMIT ALTITUDE	977m
HEIGHT GAIN	745m
MAXIMUM GRADIENT	13%
AVERAGE GRADIENT	7.5%

MAX GRADIENT **13%**

9.9km

49 Mare de Déu del Far

You get two climbs for the price of one here: first, the Coll de Condreu, and following that the ride to the summit at Mare de Déu del Far (which translates as 'Our Lady of the Lighthouse'). Heading south from Sant Esteve d'en Bas, the journey starts on the C-153 just outside the town; exactly where is not obvious, so I'm marking it as the point where a farm track intersects the road. From here, you begin to gain altitude as the road rises into the forest for 10 kilometres of very agreeable 5% gradient. With just two hairpins towards the end and no sharp ramps, the Coll de Condreu isn't much to write home about, and with very few breaks in the shroud of trees you'll only get the briefest flashes of a view. Once you reach the apex, you leave the main road and turn left to continue south on the narrow track for the final 4.5 kilometres to the finish. The first two undulate a little then lead to a short, sharp descent to the base of the final ramp. From here, you have uninterrupted climbing to the end; nothing savage, but certainly a little tougher than the lower slopes as you close in on the sanctuary. And this is why you are here: not only is there a restaurant, but carrying on through the courtyard to the very edge of the giant bluff, you will find yourself at just the most remarkable viewpoint.

FACTFILE

DIRECTIONS: Head south from Sant Esteve d'en Bas on the C-153, pass the turn to els Hostalets then shortly after start at the junction with a farm track.

SUMMIT ALTITUDE	1088m
HEIGHT GAIN	592m
MAXIMUM GRADIENT	13%
AVERAGE GRADIENT	4%

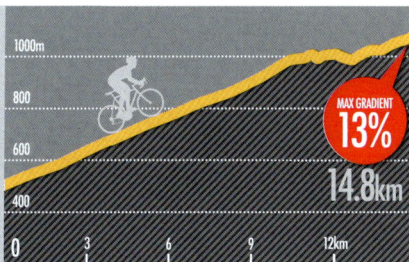

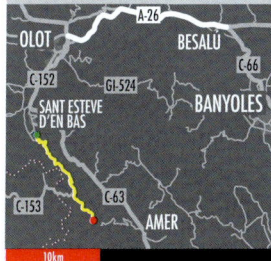

MAX GRADIENT 13%

14.8km

OLOT
BESALÚ
BANYOLES
SANT ESTEVE D'EN BAS
AMER
A-26
C-152
GI-524
C-66
C-63
C-153
10km

SANT ESTEVE D'EN BAS
C-63
LES PLANES D'HOSTOLES
COLL DE CONDREU
C-153
AMER

50 Sant Martí Sacalm

The gradient on this climb is so uniform, so perfectly consistent, I'm pretty sure I didn't change gear until the last hundred metres. Eight kilometres of metronomic perfection starts as you exit the back of Amer via a very slightly stiffer start following the signs to Sant Martí Sacalm. A firm favourite of the pros who train around here, it's the perfect venue for a 20-minute (or more like 40 for mortals) climbing test. While it's not littered with hairpins, it continually turns this way and that on a tough but far-from-savage pitch which weaves across the forested hillside. Sweeping through the corners, the key to this climb is to find that sweet spot, that climbing speed that you can maintain for the duration; stick to it and never deviate. On occasions, there are breaks in the trees where you can catch sight of the ever-improving views, but for the most part you are trapped in a tunnel of foliage, just you and your pedalling in search of the summit. If you have gauged it just right, and it does take some practice, you will arrive at the small clearing that houses the sanctuary with an empty tank. To finish the job, there's just the sharp kicker to the finish in the shadow of the bluff where high above you looms the summit of climb number 49, Mare de Déu del Far.

FACTFILE

DIRECTIONS: Leave the C-63 in Amer and follow the signs to St. Martí Sacalm on Av. del Far. At the T-junction turn right then start the climb at the next turn left.

SUMMIT ALTITUDE	816m
HEIGHT GAIN	604m
MAXIMUM GRADIENT	15%
AVERAGE GRADIENT	7.2%

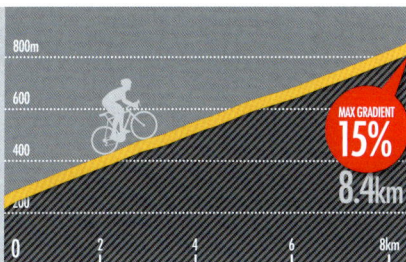

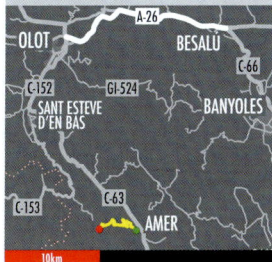

MAX GRADIENT
15%

8.4km

OLOT
BESALÚ
A-26
C-66
C-152
GI-524
SANT ESTEVE
D'EN BAS
BANYOLES
C-153
C-63
AMER

10km

MARE DE DÉU
DEL FAR
C-63
SANT MARTÍ
SACALM
AMER

The first climb that comes to mind when you think of cycling around Girona is likely to be Rocacorba. It has hotels, clothing and exclusive cycling clubs named after it, but how it has attracted so much hype, I'll never understand. This climb on the other hand, this climb IS worth the hype, and in my opinion it is the best in the region: incredible to ride, some tasty gradients, and views at the top that knock Rocacorba out of the water. The first eight kilometres are fast, so slap it in the big ring and get some speed up. Starting on a 2% slope and increasing to around 4%, you will be almost halfway before the real climbing starts. Abruptly, 4% turns to 7%, and now you'll want to change down as you follow the twisting path up through the forest. It's packed with a multitude of ramps and small descents, so just when you feel the gradient bite you are usually treated to a small recovery drop before going hard again. Up and down like an ECG, you close in on the last two kilometres which are the toughest, but the views – just wow. Breaking free from the trees, the road navigates around the rocky summit to reveal a jaw-dropping panorama across the snow-capped Pyrenees, AND at the top there is an amazing café where you can sit and soak it in for hours.

FACTFILE

DIRECTIONS: Head north from the N-260 on to the GIV-5238 towards Cabanelles then take the left turn on to the GIP-5237 to start the climb.

SUMMIT ALTITUDE	1108m
HEIGHT GAIN	908m
MAXIMUM GRADIENT	12%
AVERAGE GRADIENT	5.1%

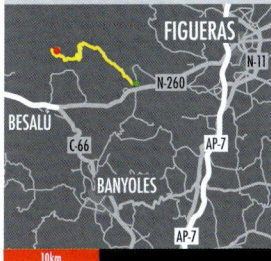

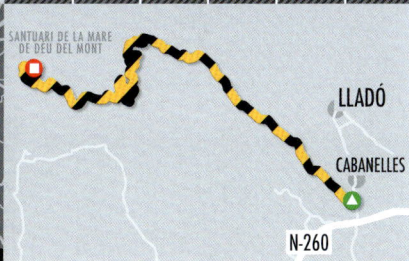

MAX GRADIENT 12%

18km

FIGUERAS

N-11

N-260

BESALÚ

C-66

AP-7

BANYOLES

AP-7

10km

SANTUARI DE LA MARE DE DÉU DEL MONT

LLADÓ

CABANELLES

N-260

52 Coll de Pal

This is an absolutely stunning road that climbs immersed in the surrounding peaks on a deathly quiet quest for high altitude. Tracing the path of and sometimes actually in the shadow of the giant viaducts that carry the highway above you, head north through the valley on a consistently pitched and at times testing slope. With kilometre after kilometre of 7, 8 and even 9% average, it's no walk in the park, but also never terribly hard. As the C-16 above you heads into a tunnel and off towards Andorra, your path turns east to face the towering peaks ahead. Twisting around the forested contours, dipping in and out of the shelter of the trees, you continue to gain altitude. Passing the Mirador de la Devesa, there are still eight kilometres left to climb, but from here on there's a noticeable easing of the slope. Gradients of 8% turn to 5 and 6% as you continue to weave through the forest, then with 2.5 kilometres left you pass through what are hopefully open gates and your surroundings change. The forested slopes are replaced by scree and exposed rock as the road, now lined with snow poles, takes you above 2,000 metres. In ever-more spectacular surroundings, the summit arrives at a large plateau, marked with a diminutive sign exposed and alone on the barren tundra.

FACTFILE

DIRECTIONS: The climb leaves the northern edge of Bagà from the junction of Av. Reina Elisenda and the BV-4024 at the 0km marker.

SUMMIT ALTITUDE	2080m
HEIGHT GAIN	1253m
MAXIMUM GRADIENT	12%
AVERAGE GRADIENT	6.7%

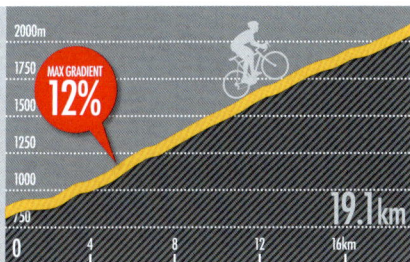

MAX GRADIENT **12%**

19.1 km

N-260

GUARDIOLA DE BERGUEDÀ
BAGÀ
LA POBLA DE LILLET
C-16
CERCS
C-26

10km

TÚNEL DEL CADÍ
COLL DE PAL
GRÉIXER
BAGÀ
C-16

53 Coll de Pradell

I do a fair bit of research before I head off on my trips, but I fell well short when studying this road. I did recall seeing a lot of red (steep gradient) on the profile, but didn't look any closer to see exactly how red it was. On reflection, I should have looked closer, as this red was actually a prolonged stretch of 20% gradient, and, I can't lie, I was THIS close to walking. It's a good while before you reach this hideous ramp, as you start the climb by leaving the C-16 south of Guardiola de Berguedà and turning west to ease up the first six kilometres beneath a monumental bluff ahead, before turning left towards Vallcebre. Passing the breathtaking Mirador de Cap-deig, there is a short drop into the village and then it's game on. This isn't the killer bit, not yet, but the next three kilometres average over 10% already and pose a substantial test. Pass the Llac de Tumi, turn left and then you see it. Ahead of you, slate-grey asphalt turns to off-white concrete, and the slope just ramps up like a ski jump. Soon reaching 20% and rough as hell, its viciousness peaks just before a pair of switchbacks; if you reach them without stopping, then congratulations. From here on, although not as brutal, the finale is never easy and will have you grovelling all the way to the end.

FACTFILE

DIRECTIONS: Start from the point where the B-400 leaves the C-16 heading west, signposted Vallcebre, Saldes and Gósol.

SUMMIT ALTITUDE	1728m
HEIGHT GAIN	1031m
MAXIMUM GRADIENT	20%
AVERAGE GRADIENT	7%

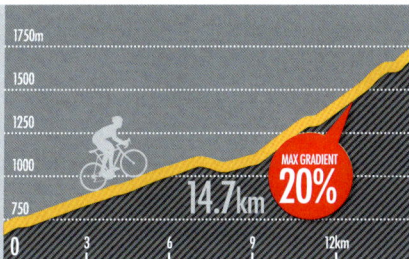

14.7km

MAX GRADIENT 20%

1750m · 1500 · 1250 · 1000 · 750

0 · 3 · 6 · 9 · 12km

N-260

BAGA · GUARDIOLA DE BERGUEDA · LA POBLA DE LILLET

C-16

CERCS

C-26

10km

GUARDIOLA DE BERGUEDA

B-400

VALLCEBRE

C-16

54 Coll de La Creueta

This is a long, steady climb – in fact, if you were to start in Guardiola de Berguedà, it would measure over 30 kilometres, but its true base lies in La Pobla de Lillet. From here, the journey to the top is a mere 21 kilometres, kicking off with the only tough bit of gradient you will face, a single kilometre of 8–9% slope before the road then drops down past the cement museum and the remains of its brutalist buildings built into the mountainside. From here on, it's up all the way, mostly around the 5–6% mark, with some stretches of 7% but nothing that will stress you. At 11 kilometres, you pass through Castellar de n'Hug which marks the end of the forested lower slopes and the start of the exposed upper slopes. Unfortunately, when I rode it, it was under rapidly darkening skies, and such is my phobia of being the tallest thing on an empty mountain in a thunderstorm, I began to pay less attention to the road and more to just how vulnerable I was now that any vegetational protection had vanished. With the horizon a line of bald, rolling hills, the ever-decreasing slope fades rapidly over its final kilometres to deliver you to the spartan summit, where I made a rapid U-turn and fled back to the lower slopes.

FACTFILE

DIRECTIONS: Start from the junction of the B-402 and BV-4031 and head north, following the signs to Castellar de n'Hug and La Molina.

SUMMIT ALTITUDE	1921m
HEIGHT GAIN	1048m
MAXIMUM GRADIENT	11%
AVERAGE GRADIENT	4.9%

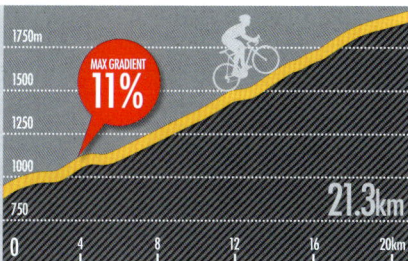

MAX GRADIENT
11%

21.3km

The Hardest Grand Tour Climb

In 1999, in a bid to draw the cycling world's attention away from the Grand Tours of Italy and France and focus it squarely on the Vuelta, the organisers of the tour of Spain introduced us all to the mighty Alto de l'Angliru. With this masterstroke, they rapidly escalated what was already becoming an arms race to find ever steeper roads, and in the process changed the *parcours* of the big events forever.

There have of course been insane mountain climbs on the routes of the Grand Tours ever since Henri Desgrange sent the pioneering participants of the 1910 Tour de France over the Col du Tourmalet. Giants such as the Stelvio Pass, Col du Galibier and Col de l'Iseran have witnessed heroics for generations, but somehow these high-altitude passes

weren't quite enough, and as modern gearing facilitated the use of steeper gradients, the search for more vicious inclines began.

The Giro d'Italia was the first to turn up the heat by sending its riders up the Mortirolo from Mazzo di Valtellina in 1991 (it had climbed the easy side the year before, but that is nothing compared to this one). This is a savage road, an absolute leg-breaker; a dope-fuelled Lance Armstrong said it was the hardest thing he'd ever ridden.

Determined to retake the crown, the Vuelta a España organisers swatted the Mortirolo aside and restored balance with the Angliru. This now-infamous road took the peloton to new levels of suffering in order to provide the essential publicity for the race and

entertainment for the sadistic cycling fans who would line the climb in their thousands. So brutal are its slopes that it led the then director of the Kelme cycling team, Vicente Belda, to utter the famous line, 'What do they want? Blood?' On a later insertion, the British rider David Millar simply refused to cross the line at the summit in protest at its use and in doing so eliminated himself from the event. Any protests fell on deaf ears, though, because the fans' lust for blood had been quenched and now they wanted more, much more.

In 2007, the horror the fans craved was duly quenched when the Giro d'Italia unveiled the stupendous Monte Zoncolan: 10 kilometres of cruel hairpins the likes of which we'd never seen before, and which wrestled the title back to Italy. The battle was seemingly over. I mean, no one could really expect there to ever be anything

harder than the Zoncolan, right? To send riders up a climb any worse would be inhumane, wouldn't it? Well, in 2017, a road appeared on the Vuelta route that on paper appeared to break the mould yet again. Would it – could it – really be harder? There was only one way to find out for sure: to go and ride it.

First, though, I have to weigh up the other contenders. How did they really feel to climb? Which of them was really the toughest?

Let's start with the Angliru, which I first tackled in 2014. The day I arrived I was fresh, eager and as excited as a puppy in a toilet roll factory. The first half is indeed tough, but it's manageable, then there's a flat section, an interlude where you can grab a drink before the real action begins. Passing the large poster of the late José María Jiménez (the first rider to win at the top), the 20% gradient starts. It's not 20% the whole way up, but there are enough double-digit sectors that my speed soon began to slow to a walking pace. Back in 2014, I was armed with a 39x27, and as I'd never been beaten before on this gear, I had no inclination that I would be that day. I was wrong. With roughly three kilometres left to climb, the road bends left and you enter the stretch known as the Cueña les Cabres and it's a ramp of pure terror. Even employing some extreme zigzagging back and forth, I knew I was not going to make it and, just before my knees were about to snap, down went my foot. This was the hardest thing I'd ever faced on two wheels and having never been forced to walk before I was in shock. I knew right away I'd have to return with a smaller gear (which I did). For now, though, this was, this had to be, the hardest Grand Tour climb ever.

Next, it was time for a date with the Zoncolan. While researching the climbs of the Dolomites in the summer of 2018, I rolled up to the bottom eager to compare it with the Angliru. Could it be even harder, as was claimed? I was better prepared this time and came armed with a more sensible lowest gear of 34x28. Would it be enough? It was, JUST, but

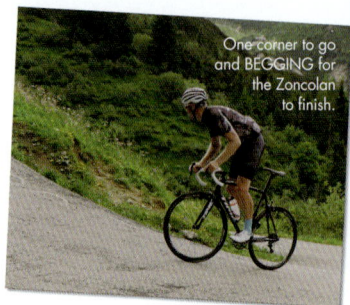
One corner to go and BEGGING for the Zoncolan to finish.

my backside didn't touch the saddle for about six kilometres. Its constant, relentless 15–16% slope wears you down both physically and mentally.

On a classic climb such as say Alpe d'Huez, the road usually eases back through the bends allowing you to spin for a while, to take a short break, but the bends on the Zoncolan, they are even steeper than the straights. There is just nowhere to rest, nowhere to hide, until with about three kilometres to go where there is the slight descent before you pass through the tunnels into the grandstand finish. By this point you are simply begging for it to end, which is why although it lacks prolonged periods over 20%, its relentlessness is what makes it harder than the Angliru. At the top, just as I'd done on the Angliru, I proclaimed the case closed; there will never be a tougher Grand Tour climb than that, it's simply not possible. Or is it?

The following summer, I visited northern Spain to pay a visit to the road the Vuelta organisers had unveiled on their 2017 edition: Los Machucos. Their bid to reclaim the top spot had resulted in the unearthing of a truly mind-boggling

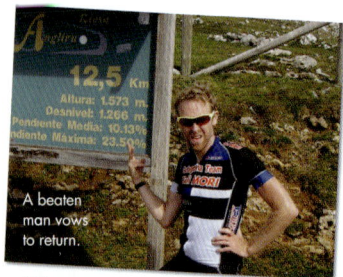
A beaten man vows to return.

THE HARDEST GRAND TOUR CLIMB

ascent. As I approached the start hidden deep in the Cantabrian mountains, my stomach was filled with butterflies. Excitement or nerves? There's some tough riding to get through before you even reach the actual climb which starts just past the village of Bustabaldo as you turn left, cross a small river then ramp up into the madness. My 34x28 which had been OK up the Zoncolan was totally insufficient here. I didn't stop, but at times I needed a more accurate device than my cycle computer to detect any forward movement.

Early on, you are hit by a series of viscous ramps, each of which smashes your legs up, and then you reach the big one: a monumental stretch of simply ludicrous 20–30% gradient. Oh, and there is more, much more. Once through a very welcome mid-climb hiatus, you appear to be riding towards the towering rocks ahead but with no obvious way through. It looks impossible for the

What horror awaits?

Los Machucos CALSECA

road to escape the fortress of rock that surrounds you, but Los Machucos somehow does. Enter the infamous concrete switchbacks. 20%, 25%, maybe even steeper: this is how you will get through the forest and escape the valley. If you weren't laughing, you'd be crying by now because it had stopped being fun a long time ago. Leaving these bends, it still goes on, but I dared not look up. I would not – could not – give in though, and no matter how slowly I travelled I was going to reach the top. Eventually, in the eerie solitude of these secluded mountains, I made it.

Los Machucos takes suffering to the next level. By comparison, the slopes of the Angliru and Zoncolan, as savage and unforgiving as they are, suddenly seem quite sedate. My list of the hardest Grand Tour climbs now has a new name at the top, until, that is, the sadistic race planners find something even more difficult on which the world's best riders can entertain us.

I can't wait!

Los Machucos. 25% ribbed concrete hairpins. INSANE.

VALENCIA

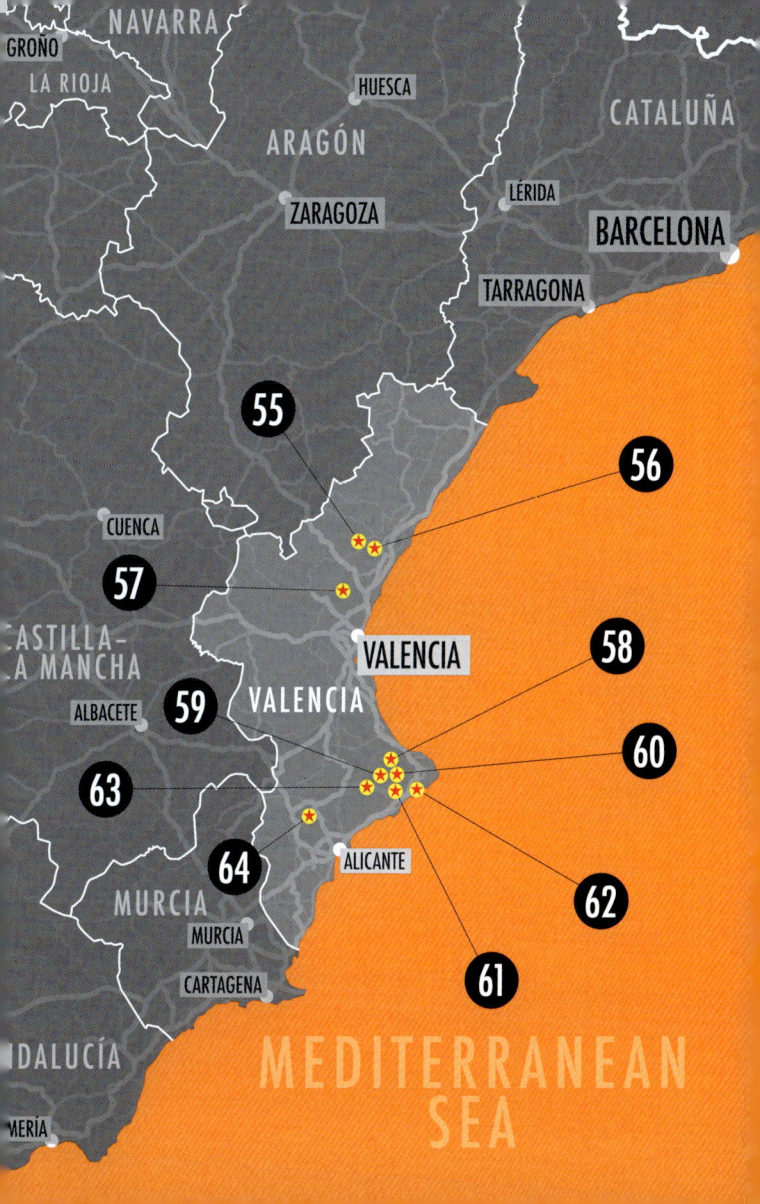

55 Puerto de Almedíjar

Quiet? It felt as if I was the only person on the planet at times on this climb. In a four-hour window on this ride, I saw three cars, a van and a horse, so if you want quiet roads then you will just love it around here. Of the two sides to this pass, I have chosen the western flank heading in roughly a straight line north-east through Almedíjar. The surface is rough and ready, although of course you may be lucky and this could have changed by now, but at the time of riding it added to the road's backwater feeling. Starting on a steady 5% slope and then easing way back, it's not until about halfway that there is anything even remotely testing as the average tips up to hover around 6%. Predominantly trapped in scrubby woodland, your views of the surrounding hills are mostly restricted, but as you climb higher you are afforded clearer lines of sight. With seven kilometres under your wheels, you'll feel an increase in the effort required to pedal, and the final kilometre – which averages close to 9% – may well be quite a shock. Now high above the green interlocking hills, the summit arrives, a mini canyon carved through the mountain's peak, as you cross a line on the floor marked with '2RD'.

FACTFILE

DIRECTIONS: Start the climb on the CV-200 from the junction where the CV-2183 joins from the south.

SUMMIT ALTITUDE	793m
HEIGHT GAIN	453m
MAXIMUM GRADIENT	10%
AVERAGE GRADIENT	5%

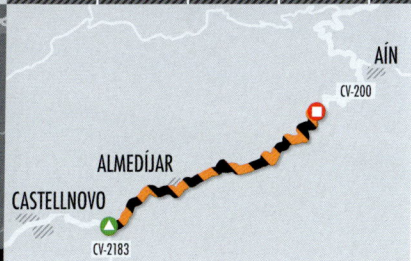

MAX GRADIENT **10%**

9km

56 Puntal de l'Aljub

This climb starts on a standard, gently sloping wide and well-surfaced road, then finishes all kinds of crazy as you exit the main road to head for the antennae. Turning into and then navigating around Eslida, the first half of the ascent is set on a reasonably stiff incline through the town, then eases back a touch as it begins to wind relentlessly into the hills. With no more than a handful of metres between bends, the first five kilometres are a joy as you follow the road's flow upwards. This part of the climb comes to an end at the summit of the Port d'Eslida where, if you had any sense, you'd continue straight on down the other side – but I do hope that's not the decision you make. To continue the adventure, take the much smaller road here that heads west deeper into the hills and which will deliver you to the true summit – capped with its array of antennae high on the horizon. After a kilometre of undulation, the VERY rough surface then sinks its teeth into your legs and ramps up to over 10% and never relents. The views are magnificent as you fight your bike around the hairpins that populate the final stretch. With a lot of gradient over 15%, and in places approaching 20%, it's a hell of a fight, but oh-so-worth-it.

FACTFILE

DIRECTIONS: Start the climb in Eslida by taking the CV-219 heading south-west, following the signs to Chovar and Soneja.

SUMMIT ALTITUDE	944m
HEIGHT GAIN	599m
MAXIMUM GRADIENT	17%
AVERAGE GRADIENT	7.3%

MAX GRADIENT **17%**

8.2km

CV-202 ONDA
CV-200
CV-215
ESLIDA
CV-200
SEGORBE
CV-219
A-23
10km

CV-223
ESLIDA
PORT D'ESLIDA
CV-219
CHÓVAR

57 Alt del Pi

Heading though the Parc Natural de la Serra Calderona, this climb, which can be tackled from a number of directions and start points, is very close to the hearts of all riders in the Valencia area. The closet big ascent to the city, it's where they all head to gain some serious altitude and because of this you'll always cross paths with other cyclists on its slopes. I've chosen to take the route up through the village of Segart, and upon leaving the valley the road begins with four very steady kilometres. Lulling you into a false sense of security, this very mild opening ends abruptly when you reach Segart and from here the following three kilometres are nasty: averaging 9%, 13% and then 9%, they really sting as you rapidly rise above the surrounding hills. Following this barrage of steep slopes, you are then afforded some rest before a final tough kilometre to the eventual peak which lies just after you turn left on to the CV-3342. Don't stop here though as there is a little treat just round the corner that you MUST check out. Continue west, drop down slightly then double back on yourself to take the left turn for a further 1,500 metres of climbing on a super-smooth road that's close to 20% in places on its way to the antennae on top of the Alt del Pi.

FACTFILE

DIRECTIONS: Start the climb on the CV-329 from the roundabout just west of the A-23 motorway.

SUMMIT ALTITUDE	716m
HEIGHT GAIN	616m
MAXIMUM GRADIENT	18%
AVERAGE GRADIENT	5.6%

MAX GRADIENT **18%**

11km

58 Coll de la Vall de Ebo

Second in popularity in these parts only to the Coll de Rates, this wonderful road was thick with riders the day I arrived. From pro teams in neat formation to holidaymakers and countless athletes trying to set PBs, its modestly pitched slopes were buzzing with activity. The base lies just south of Pego where you turn west from the CV-715 and, following the signs to the Vall de Ebo, begin to climb between the walls on either side of you. From a gentle start, you settle into close to nine kilometres of very steady climbing that never exceeds 7% – hence its popularity. Writhing around beautiful villas and olive groves, the first couple of kilometres are the busiest, then after a short time hidden in trees the road breaks free to reveal the glorious views it is famous for. Climbing through the exposed rock, the narrow road, lined with the region's typical white concrete bollards, heads into the mountains via a constant stream of sweeping corners. Naturally, the higher you climb, the grander the vista, then following one final look out you arrive at the rather underwhelming summit. Whether you choose to attack this climb full gas or simply head out for a leisurely pedal, it is just about the perfect venue for a ride.

FACTFILE

DIRECTIONS: Leave the CV-715 just south of Pego and follow the CV-712 west towards Vall de Ebo.

SUMMIT ALTITUDE	543m
HEIGHT GAIN	465m
MAXIMUM GRADIENT	7%
AVERAGE GRADIENT	5.4%

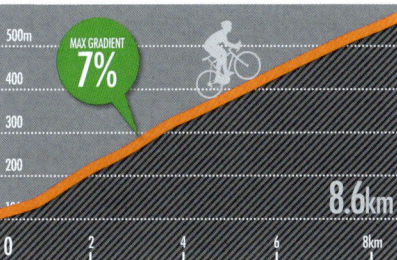

MAX GRADIENT
7%

8.6km

59 Coll de Garga

Although I rode this climb east to west, I kind of wish I'd ridden it the other way – I will have to go back one day to tick off that ascent. The eastern side is still brilliant, however, and – at 11 kilometres – is also pretty long for these parts. The ascent starts with a steady straight approach to the first of many challenges ahead; a series of switchbacks that takes you past the village of La Plana. No tough gradient yet, apart from in the corners, then it's on to Campell and Fleix as the road becomes narrower and narrower. Between houses and fruit trees you continue to rise through the Laguar valley and the next settlement in your path is Benimaurell, a small hillside village that holds a special surprise. Turning left as soon as you reach the first houses, and following the sign to the village centre, the slope soon kicks up steeply – once past a tiny plaza, it ramps right up to about 20%. Barely wide enough for the smallest of cars, the 100-metre stretch of wicked gradient in this tiny urban canyon delivers you to a T-junction where you head left in search of the summit. The higher slopes are now much tougher to ride, with the final three kilometres all averaging close to 9% with many prolonged periods of 15%, before you can rest at the top and enjoy the spectacular panoramic views.

FACTFILE

DIRECTIONS: Start the climb from the junction of the CV-715 and CV-721, heading south-west on the latter following the sign to Vall de Laguar.

SUMMIT ALTITUDE	759m
HEIGHT GAIN	654m
MAXIMUM GRADIENT	20%
AVERAGE GRADIENT	6.1%

10.8km

MAX GRADIENT 20%

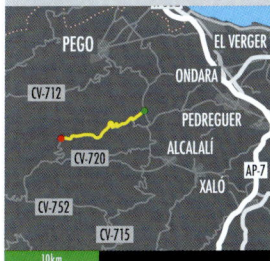

The Coll de Rates is to the Costa Blanca what Sa Calobra is to Mallorca, or Teide is to Tenerife: it's THE signature climb that everyone makes a beeline for. It is neither long nor exceptionally hard, but over the years it has built a legend which cannot be ignored. Naturally, a climb with this sort of reputation demands a little more attention from the rider, meaning you empty your water bottles at the bottom, down a caffeine gel and hit it full gas until the very top. Heading south from Parcent, the first four kilometres sway this way and that, gently climbing up the ridge, starting on a steady 4% and only just reaching 5%. Following a tight left-hand hairpin at the four-kilometre mark, you swing round and now the slope bites some more as the pitch ramps up close to 8% and you head up the side of the mountain in one direct line to the final corner. With almost uninterrupted views out across the valley to the sea, this is a glorious stretch of road which after its single tough kilometre reverts to the steadier 5% slope. Don't back off though; change up the gears and keep the pressure on all the way to the summit so you can reward yourself with a massive cake and an ice-cold beer while soaking up the views from the conveniently located restaurant that's impossible to ride past.

F A C T F I L E

DIRECTIONS: Head south out of Parcent on the CV-715 and start to climb after the junction with the CV-720.

SUMMIT ALTITUDE	628m
HEIGHT GAIN	354m
MAXIMUM GRADIENT	9%
AVERAGE GRADIENT	5.2%

MAX GRADIENT
9%

6.8km

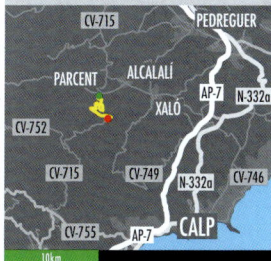

I tacked this climb on to the end of a big day in the saddle because I'd seen the riders in the Tour of Valencia head up it a few weeks earlier and it looked like a real killer. By the time I got to the top, though, I wished I had just ridden straight past. WOW. What you are faced with is five kilometres of over 12% average gradient, which actually makes it sound a lot easier than it really is. Maybe I had tired legs at the end of a seven-hour ride, but still, it was agony. The first part from the main road up past a few secluded villas, that is OK, but then with four kilometres to go it gets NASTY. With barely a moment's respite, the slope kicks up to assume its angle of attack of between 15 and 20% all the way to the end. If you look on Google Street View, it's just about the only road in the region that hasn't been photographed, and if you want more evidence of its severity, then go check out the footage from stage 4 of the 2020 Tour of Valencia. By the time I reached the top, the sun was beginning to go down and I had to rest just a little before shredding my brake pads and setting my rims on fire on the hair-raising return back to the base. I know I may not have done that good a job of selling this one, but for those who love a challenge, this is exactly what you've been looking for.

FACTFILE

DIRECTIONS: There are three ways to start the climb and I have chosen the middle one. Head north from the CV-755 following the signs to Serra de Bèrnia.

SUMMIT ALTITUDE	706m
HEIGHT GAIN	640m
MAXIMUM GRADIENT	20%
AVERAGE GRADIENT	12.5%

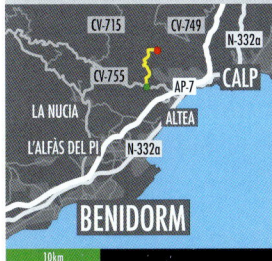

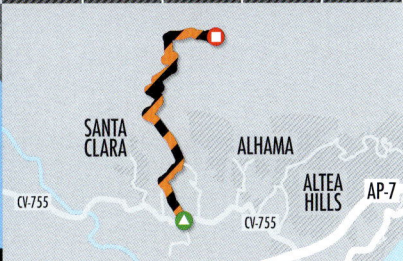

MAX GRADIENT **20%**

5.1km

62 Cumbre del Sol

If you are looking for a view of the Costa Blanca to rival the one you had out of your aeroplane's window, then this is where you need to come. A short ride up the coast from Calp, the classic side of this ascent begins in Alcàsar and, although only 3.7 kilometres long, it packs a mighty punch. The first kilometre of the climb averages a gruelling 12% and snakes out of town, past the walls of increasingly large villas. The second kilometre begins with a slightly shallower stretch, sweeping around a right-hand bend then into a long, straight, tree-lined ramp where the fantastic views begin. All the way up this punishing avenue, you can soak in the scenes of the coastal towns and azure waters over to your right which are spectacular enough to stop you in your tracks. Reaching a roundabout adorned with an abstract sail sculpture, it's time to start the last kilometre with its more vicious gradient past even more opulent properties boasting even grander views. Now heading north, you arrive at the final junction, a harsh left-hand turn that ushers in the push for the top. The steepest gradients are to be found here as you climb up through a right-hand hairpin then all the way to the very end of the road, which also goes by the name Puig Llorença.

FACTFILE

DIRECTIONS: Leave the CV-737 at the large roundabout past the supermarket car park. At the next roundabout head left, then at the third start the climb.

SUMMIT ALTITUDE	422m
HEIGHT GAIN	362m
MAXIMUM GRADIENT	18%
AVERAGE GRADIENT	9.8%

MAX GRADIENT **18%**

3.7km

63 Puerto de Tudons

Heading inland from your coastal residence, there's no better start to the day than these sumptuous 17 kilometres of moderate 5% gradient winding into the Aitana mountain range. You'll begin to feel the slope bite by the time you reach Finestrat, which is where I placed the start of the climb, at the junction of the CV-761 and the CV-758. Starting to rise, you head north-west towards the town of Sella, turning right when you join the CV-770 to continue on its immaculate surface that comes equipped with wonderful bike lanes. Sella sits elevated on a mound dead in your path at roughly the five-kilometre mark, forcing the road to squirm through a series of bends and increase in severity for a short time to reach it. Upon leaving town, the bike lanes that had lined the road disappear and as the scenery becomes wilder the climb begins to twist and turn more frequently. With 11 kilometres covered, you reach the stiffest part of the journey where the slope touches 10% around some of the tighter corners. Now packed with bends, the final section is great fun to ride and as the gradient returns to a more sedate 5% you can pick up speed to finish like a pro at the clearing that marks the summit.

FACTFILE

DIRECTIONS: Start from the junction of the CV-761 and CV-758 at the western side of Finestrat and head north-west.

SUMMIT ALTITUDE	1024m
HEIGHT GAIN	740m
MAXIMUM GRADIENT	10%
AVERAGE GRADIENT	4.4%

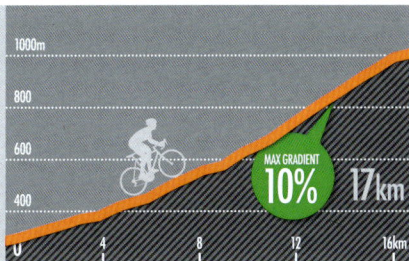

MAX GRADIENT 10% 17km

'Right,' I said to Nick and Paul who I was travelling with. 'This one is only short. I'm going to attack it from the base and I'll see you at the top.' WHAT A MISTAKE THAT WAS. This classic Vuelta torture chamber, first used to punish the riders back in 1998, may only be four kilometres long, but what an evil four kilometres they are. The climb starts after a slight dip in the road, then as you pass a junction on your left and as a white wall starts on your right, it ramps up. The first few hundred metres aren't actually that steep, but once you reach the 20% gradient sign, from there on it's murder. It's not 20% all the way – that would be too much – but it never drops below 10%, and in reality it hovers at around 15% for most of the next three and a half kilometres. Heading south through the sparse woodland, there are a few kinks in direction, but no hairpins as you ride across the multitude of faded names and offers of encouragement painted on the tarmac. Each of the 20% ramps slows your progress to walking pace, but if, like me, you have decided to ride hard, you can't give in to them; you must fight on. The summit arrives abruptly at the end of the final killer ramp where you'll feel like coughing up a lung before of course pressing on in search of more fun.

FACTFILE

DIRECTIONS: Head south from Castalla on Avenida de Petrer and start the climb after the small dip in the road before the turn on your left.

SUMMIT ALTITUDE	1097m
HEIGHT GAIN	437m
MAXIMUM GRADIENT	20%
AVERAGE GRADIENT	11.1%

MAX GRADIENT **20%**

3.9km

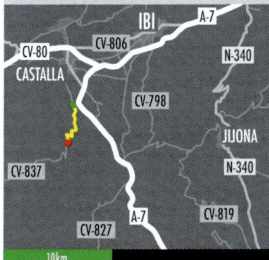

SISTEMA CENTRAL

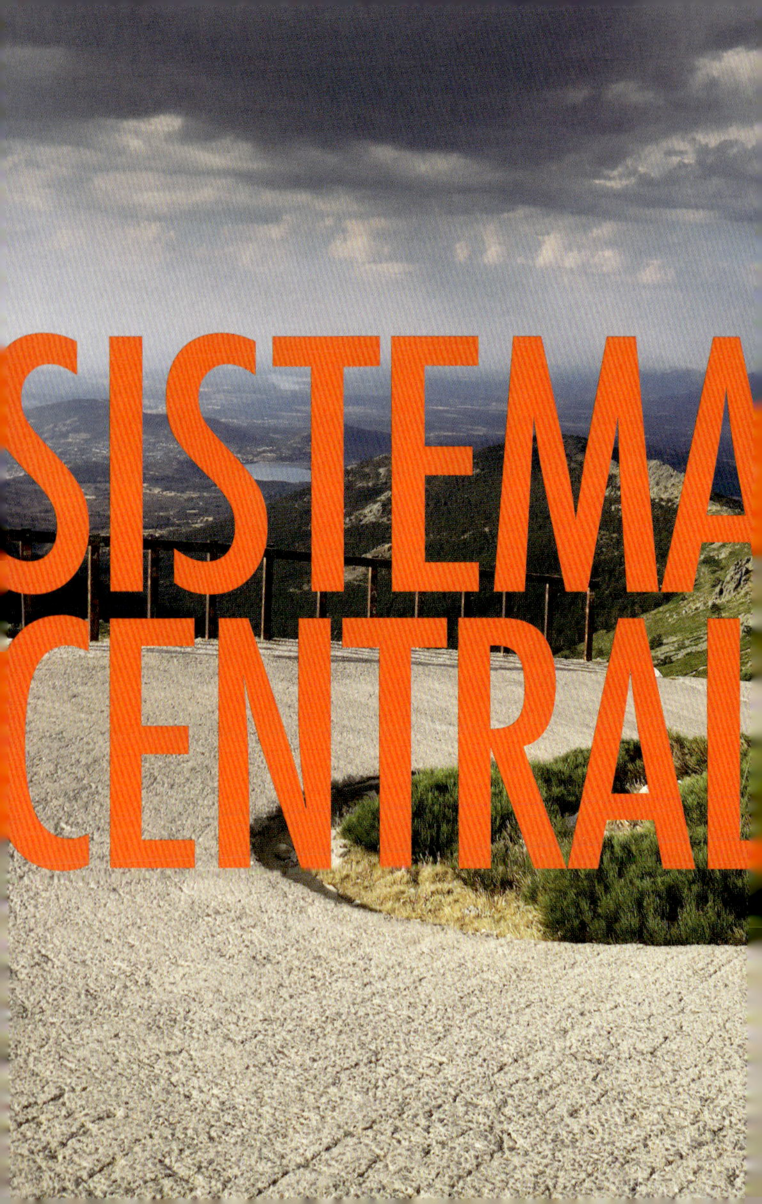

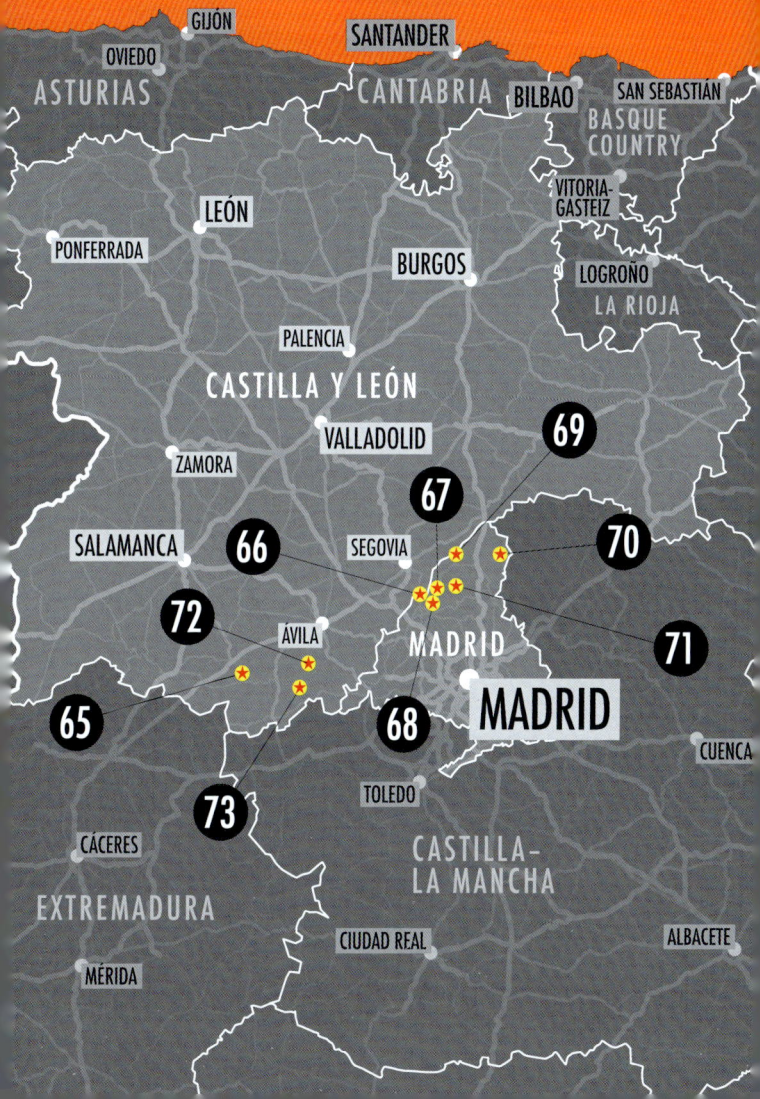

BAY OF BISCAY

GIJÓN
SANTANDER
OVIEDO
ASTURIAS
CANTABRIA
BILBAO
SAN SEBASTIÁN
BASQUE
COUNTRY
VITORIA-
GASTEIZ
LEÓN
PONFERRADA
BURGOS
LOGROÑO
LA RIOJA
PALENCIA
CASTILLA Y LEÓN
VALLADOLID
ZAMORA
69
67
SALAMANCA
66
SEGOVIA
70
72
ÁVILA
MADRID
71
65
68
MADRID
CUENCA
TOLEDO
73
CASTILLA–
LA MANCHA
CÁCERES
EXTREMADURA
MÉRIDA
CIUDAD REAL
ALBACETE

65 Puerto de la Peña Negra

Depositing my family at the open-air pool in Piedrahíta so they could splash around in the cool water, I set off up this climb in the baking 36-degree heat. Leaving town, you face just over 14 kilometres of moderately pitched slope that sways skywards into the Sierra de Gredos mountains to open up simply colossal views. With a maximum gradient of only 9% and an average just below 6%, it's not a climb that will kill the legs if you don't want it to – there's nothing here to be afraid of at all. A couple of kilometres after leaving Piedrahíta, you pass through Pesquera then continue across the wooded hillside, which could for a while offer a modicum of shelter from a blazing sun. At the seven-kilometre mark the trees disappear and from here to the top you traverse the exposed mountainside while casting your eyes north across the parched plains of Castilla y León. With just four more changes in direction through the final eight kilometres, the scenery becomes ever-more dramatic while under your wheels the gradient remains perfectly benign. Turning your back on the view, you spy the summit sign advertising its 1,909-metre altitude, but annoyingly it does not sit at the crest of the road, so to ensure you complete the ascent you must pass it by and continue over the top.

FACTFILE

DIRECTIONS: Head south out of Piedrahíta on Calle Fuera de la Villa and start the climb after the junction of Calle Barco.

SUMMIT ALTITUDE	1909m
HEIGHT GAIN	839m
MAXIMUM GRADIENT	9%
AVERAGE GRADIENT	5.9%

MAX GRADIENT **9%**

14.2km

66 Puerto de Navacerrada

There are three ways to the summit of the Puerto de Navacerrada, home to a ski station in the winter but in the summer months a magnet for cyclists from both Segovia to the north and Madrid to the south. I've chosen the route heading south from Segovia which begins to climb shortly after you pass through Real Sitio de San Ildefonso. As you leave town, you'll pass a sign telling you the summit is 17 kilometres away, but fear not, it isn't 17 kilometres of climbing, as the road undulates gradually up through Pradera de Navalhorno on a very gentle 2–3% for almost 10 kilometres. After this most placid of beginnings, and with 10 of the advertised 17 kilometres under your belt, you'll be feeling very pleased with your progress, but from here the climb gets tougher. With the pitch now increasing to around the 7% mark, you head into the first of the eight beautiful sweeping hairpins which guide the wide road though the thick forest heading into the Sierra de Guadarrama. With three kilometres to go, the final bend is negotiated and from here on it's pretty much a straight line. For the first time, there are some breaks in the surrounding conifers allowing you a glance back down the valley before you arrive at the vast intersection that marks the summit.

FACTFILE

DIRECTIONS: Head south out of Real Sitio de San Ildefonso on the CL-601 and start the climb from the bottom of the small descent.

SUMMIT ALTITUDE	1860m
HEIGHT GAIN	686m
MAXIMUM GRADIENT	10%
AVERAGE GRADIENT	4.2%

MAX GRADIENT **10%**

16.4km

SEGOVIA
N-110
CL-601
RASCAFRÍA
AP-61
M-604
MIRAFLORES DE LA SIERRA
CERCEDILLA
M-601
10km

REAL SITIO DE SAN ILDEFONSO
RASCAFRÍA
PRADERA DE NAVALHORNO
PARQUE NACIONAL DE LA SIERRA DE GUADARRAMA
M-604
M-611
PUERTO DE CANENCIA
M-629
PUERTO DE LOS COTOS
PUERTO DE LA MORCUERA
PUERTO DE NAVACERRADA
MIRAFLORES DE LA SIERRA

I kid you not, when I rode this climb there were a team of men sweeping and tending to its verges, seemingly to preserve its immaculate condition. The manicured tarmac, snaking up though the glorious pine forest, is so neat it's more like a Japanese ornamental garden than a public road. Some resources list the climb as another ascent of the Puerto de Navacerrada, which it does ultimately reach, but only after cresting the Puerto de Cotos first then completing the journey via a seven-kilometre plateau. To climb to the Cotos summit, it's a 14-kilometre journey south-west from Rascafría deep in the Sierra de Guadarrama on a gradient that increases incrementally as you travel. Starting on a shallow 2% and only rising as steep as 8%, it's never a hard climb, and to aid your progress further there are handy signs at each kilometre informing you of what lies ahead. There are a couple of hairpins as you inch upwards out of the valley, but on the whole the road just gently meanders beneath the tall conifers, swaying steadily as it places you into a Zen-like state. The summit finally arrives, and there's a restaurant, visitor centre and giant car park, facilities for people heading off hiking in the mountains.

FACTFILE

DIRECTIONS: Head south-west out of Rascafría on the M-604 and start the climb as you pass the entrance to the Santa María de El Paular monastery.

SUMMIT ALTITUDE	1830m
HEIGHT GAIN	674m
MAXIMUM GRADIENT	8%
AVERAGE GRADIENT	4.7%

MAX GRADIENT 8% 14.1km

68 La Bola del Mundo

This road had been right at the top of my bucket list from the very first time I saw it on TV. It's pure Vuelta madness. Three kilometres of ruthless concrete track that picks its way almost to the very summit of the Sierra de Guadarrama. The lunacy starts at the top of the Puerto de Navacerrada where you pull off the main road, ride through a jumble of buildings then kiss your saddle goodbye. On a surface of gravel-strewn ribbed concrete, you begin to grind upwards on the near-20% slope across the barren landscape for almost a kilometre before the incline eases for a while. Traversing the edge of the mountain, this maniacal road then thrashes back and forth, mercilessly steep through five tight bends that will have you fighting for both forward motion and traction. Now at well over 2,000 metres altitude, after a long straight you are faced with another brace of bends: this is the last time for any relaxation before the push for the summit. The final 500 metres to the Alto de las Guarramillas, or La Bola del Mundo, are an all-out assault on your body. Relentlessly tough, and brutally rough and debris-covered, they place you centre stage in a draw-dropping panorama as you crawl to the giant towers that mark the summit of this, a must-ride 100% Vuelta classic.

FACTFILE

DIRECTIONS: At the top of the Puerto de Navacerrada leave the road and head south on to the Calle dos Castillas, then pass between the buildings and take the first left.

SUMMIT ALTITUDE	2257m
HEIGHT GAIN	385m
MAXIMUM GRADIENT	24%
AVERAGE GRADIENT	12.4%

MAX GRADIENT **24%**

3.1km

This 11.5-kilometre ascent takes you from the base of the Lozoya valley, up to the border with Castilla y León and the ski centre set in its mountaintop paradise. There are no giant pistes here, though; instead, this winter activity hub is home to 33 kilometres of tracks where you can indulge in the art of cross-country, or Nordic, skiing. The prospect of snow at the summit when it was 35 degrees in the valley would have been heaven, but, alas, quite obviously on a baking August day, there was none. Set – as you will come to expect around here – on tarmac as smooth as a baby's backside and on an average close to 6%, this isn't a tough climb. Once away from the cafés and restaurants in Lozoya, and past the last of the village's dwellings, the road plunges into the forest where it then stays. Through a sporadic collection of hairpins, you climb lost in the trees, silent and alone, searching for light and a break from the claustrophobia of never-ending foliage. With roughly two kilometres to go, the freedom from darkness you crave arrives, and for a moment you can expand your line of sight across the valley. This glimpse of the outside world is all too brief though, as you then head back once more into the lush forest to tick off the gentle final kilometre to the summit.

FACTFILE

DIRECTIONS: Simply turn off the M-604 in Lozoya and ride north through and then out of the village following the sign to the summit.

SUMMIT ALTITUDE	1773m
HEIGHT GAIN	668m
MAXIMUM GRADIENT	12%
AVERAGE GRADIENT	5.8%

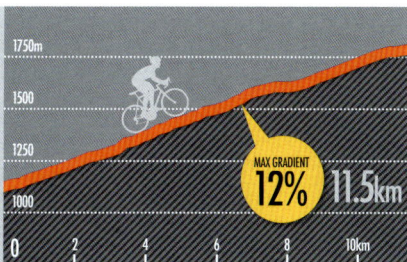

MAX GRADIENT **12%**   11.5km

N-110
N-110
LOZOYA
M-604
RASCAFRÍA
CL-601
M-604
10km

CENTRO DE ESQUÍ NÓRDICO NAVAFRÍA
REAJO ALTO
LOZOYA
M-604
M-604

70 Puerto de la Puebla

This, the last climb I rode while researching this guide at the end of two relentless weeks in the summer of 2022, was thankfully no killer because I was running on empty. Sitting on the eastern edge of the Sierra de Guadarrama amongst a collection of conservatively pitched, moderately long climbs, the rise to the Puerto de la Puebla is eight kilometres of joy. Leaving Puebla de la Sierra, trapped at the very base of the V in the valley, you start up slopes that hover mostly around the 6–7% mark. Climbing in a straight line to begin with, the first hairpins arrive after three kilometres – just a couple of them – before another long straight that takes you into a protracted right-hand bend before five more tight turns. Here, this puppy dog of a climb does bare its teeth a little as a couple of the bends pivot around seriously steep apexes. Very briefly hitting 20%, these peaks in gradient are short enough to tackle in one concerted push, getting back in the saddle in between. Altitude is gained rapidly between the bends, and through gaps in the forest you'll spy the summit above you. From the final hairpin, there's just 1,500 metres to go on a slightly shallower slope to the sign at the top which for me marked the culmination of eight years riding 100 awesome Spanish climbs.

FACTFILE

DIRECTIONS: Heading north through the centre of Puebla de la Sierra start the climb from the bridge on the corner at the centre of the village.

SUMMIT ALTITUDE	1635m
HEIGHT GAIN	481m
MAXIMUM GRADIENT	20%
AVERAGE GRADIENT	5.6%

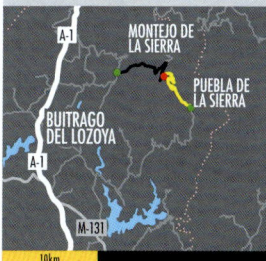

MAX GRADIENT **20%**

8.6km

71 Puerto de la Morcuera

Such are my schedules on research trips that when I arrive at a mountain which has more than one way up, I will have already decided which ascent I will ride and include, but with this climb I was able to afford myself the luxury of experiencing both sides before making my decision. I first tackled the south face from Soto del Real up through Miraflores – 17 kilometres with some significant stretches of harsh 9% slope. Then, later in the day, I rode the north side from Rascafría, which is shorter at just 11 kilometres, and a significantly shallower climb. With an average gradient of just 5% over its length compared to 7% on the south side, the route from Rascafría is comfortably the easiest, so it may surprise you that it was this side I chose to include. My reasons were threefold: first, the north face boasts more consistent views out over the valley and surrounding peaks; second, it has more hairpin bends (always a winner); and third, I fell for the vast expanse of the upper slopes as they cross the desert-like scenery before reaching the forest summit. Set on a mild 3% incline with an uninterrupted line of sight across the Guadarrama mountains, this open plateau forms a spectacular finale to a wonderful climb in a glorious part of the world.

FACTFILE

DIRECTIONS: Head south from Rascafría on Calle del Aguilón (the M-611) and start from the unmarked point after 1.4km where the road begins to rise.

SUMMIT ALTITUDE	1784m
HEIGHT GAIN	631m
MAXIMUM GRADIENT	10%
AVERAGE GRADIENT	5.8%

MAX GRADIENT **10%**

10.8km

RASCAFRÍA
M-604
CL-601
MIRAFLORES DE LA SIERRA
M-601
BECERRIL DE LA SIERRA
SOTO DEL REAL
M-608

REAL SITIO DE SAN ILDEFONSO
RASCAFRÍA
PRADERA DE NAVALHORNO
Parque Nacional de la Sierra de Guadarrama
M-604
PUERTO DE CANENCIA
M-629
M-611
PUERTO DE LA MORCUERA
PUERTO DE LOS COTOS
PUERTO DE NAVACERRADA
MIRAFLORES DE LA SIERRA

72 Puerto de Navalmoral

After cresting the summit of this climb, I rolled back a few metres to grab some photos down the valley and at the same time pay homage to the utter perfection of its new surface. It must have been laid just weeks, maybe even days, before my arrival, because it was the finest pitch-black carpet of asphalt I'd ever seen. Hats off once more to the road builders of Spain: you are masters of your craft. Top pro riders tackle this road at close to 30kph thanks to its slope never really exceeding 5%, so it's one you can enjoy romping up rather than grinding up (maybe). Starting in Burgohondo, you can split the ascent into two parts: the first almost-seven kilometres to Navalmoral which are extremely easy, and then the eight kilometres that follow which to be honest aren't much tougher. Riding into Navalmoral, you reach the Avenue de Gredos which bisects the town and, resisting the urge for a café stop, cross straight over to start the second half. This is the most rewarding part of the ride as you snake across the arid, boulder-strewn hillside that's been baked for millennia under the blazing Spanish sun. Closing in on the summit, you reach the only hairpins en route, a couple of wide, sweeping corners which allow you to soak up the magnificent views before rolling over the top.

FACTFILE

DIRECTIONS: Start the climb on the AV-900 from the T-junction with the AV-902 in Burgohondo and follow the sign north to Navalmoral.

SUMMIT ALTITUDE	1514m
HEIGHT GAIN	676m
MAXIMUM GRADIENT	7%
AVERAGE GRADIENT	4.5%

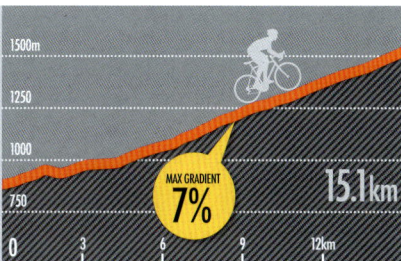

MAX GRADIENT **7%**

15.1km

73 Puerto de Mijares

The Sistema Central, or Central System, is the collection of mountain ranges running roughly east to west that divides the central part of the Iberian peninsula. From the Sierra de Guadarrama north of Madrid, all the way to the Serra de Estrela in Portugal, via the Sierra de Gredos where this magnificent pass resides, it is home to a multitude of killer roads. Starting from the south, there are three ways to begin this climb: I've chosen what is considered the classic route up through Gavilanes, and it's on this stretch you'll find the toughest gradients. Not too steep, however – they only briefly hit 10% in places on the way to the central focus of the climb, the town of Mijares. It's here the three tributaries join, and heading on there's just one way to the summit, and what a road it is. Hardly wavering from a beautifully steady 5–6% slope, the narrow pass picks its way through rugged mountain scenery via a jumble of hairpins lined almost permanently by the distinctive barrier. Once clear of what little tree cover there is lower down, the views behind you are simply sensational as you navigate through the relentless curves between exposed rock and cacti to the summit of one of THE best cycling climbs in Spain FULL STOP.

FACTFILE

DIRECTIONS: Start the climb from the junction on the CL-501 heading north on the AV-P705 following the signs to Gavilanes and Mijares.

SUMMIT ALTITUDE	1570m
HEIGHT GAIN	1106m
MAXIMUM GRADIENT	10%
AVERAGE GRADIENT	5.1%

MAX GRADIENT
10%

21.9km

ANDALUCÍA

Sierra de la Pandera – eight kilometres of wicked gradients on dire road surfaces that swagger through wild scenery to a high-altitude vantage point with a view to die for. Starting in the south, you'll first have to climb on the A-6050 via Valdepeñas de Jaén, or from the north either on the A-6050 from Los Villares via the Puerto Viejo or from Fuensanta de Martos on the JA-3301. Getting some climbing in the legs beforehand is no bad thing as you don't want to hit the 16% slopes cold, and that's what you face right off the bat. Turning from the main road there are no signs to the summit – just look for the tall gates which frame the road and indicate you are in the right place. The start is abrupt, however soon after there's a small descent followed by 1,500 metres of steadier slope. Make the most of this, because from here on it gets harder and harder. Not consistently hard, but hitting you in nasty bursts as you struggle through the coarse environment, dodging potholes and various other deformations in the surface. Reaching a peak, you'll soon realise it's not actually the finish, as ahead you'll spy the second peak which you'll reach via a precipitous drop that thankfully will give you almost enough momentum to carry you up the other side without another pedal stroke.

FACTFILE

DIRECTIONS: From the A-6050 start the climb where the small unmarked road heads east through the (hopefully) open gates.

SUMMIT ALTITUDE	1832m
HEIGHT GAIN	669m
MAXIMUM GRADIENT	18%
AVERAGE GRADIENT	8.2%

MAX GRADIENT **18%** 8.2km

A-6050
JA-3301

CASA HUERTA DE LOS OJOS

A-6050

A-316   JAÉN   A-44
MARTOS   A-6050
JA-3300
A-316   LOS VILLARES
ALCAUDETE   JA-3302
N-432   VALDEPEÑAS DE JAÉN
10km

75 Fortaleza de la Mota

This entry may seem a bit random, somewhat lost amongst the monumental mountain passes, but from the moment I saw Ethan Hayter romping across its brutal cobbles to win stage 2 of the 2021 Vuelta a Andalucía, I knew I had to pay it a visit. Alcalá la Real is just one of a multitude of Spanish hilltop towns, all packed with viciously steep roads and usually topped with a large castle – in this case, the 13th-century Fortaleza de la Mota. That isn't extraordinary, but the fact that this road (if you can call it that) has been used multiple times for a finish to a race, well, that is. The route to the summit begins up Calle Real with 500 metres of part tarmac, part paving, getting steeper and steeper and approaching the 20% mark as it squeezes between the encroaching houses. At a triangular junction, you bend left and then take the first right into the madness of the cobbled finale. Set on small, slippery stones, neat yet randomly packed, the viciously steep medieval road winds around the base of the castle. In one large arc you bounce from stone to stone to the gates which unfortunately mark your finish (if you obey the sign), even though the race route carried on for a further 150 metres into the castle grounds.

FACTFILE

DIRECTIONS: In the middle of Alcalá la Real, leave Calle de la Tejuela and head south-west on Calle Real following the sign to Fortaleza de la Mota.

SUMMIT ALTITUDE	1015m
HEIGHT GAIN	94m
MAXIMUM GRADIENT	20%
AVERAGE GRADIENT	12%

MAX GRADIENT **20%**

780m

ALCAUDETE

JA-3302

VALDEPEÑAS DE JAÉN

CASTILLO DE LOCUBÍN

N-432

ALCALÁ LA REAL

A-339

ALMEDINILLA

N-432

A-403

10km

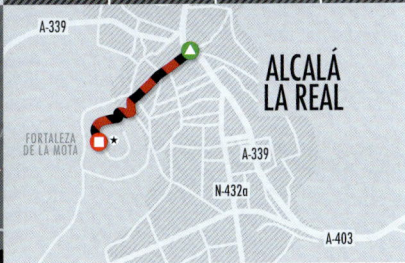

A-339

ALCALÁ LA REAL

FORTALEZA DE LA MOTA

A-339

N-432a

A-403

76 Cáñar

Quite short but extremely rewarding, these 7.5 kilometres of constant hairpins link the town of Órgiva in the valley to the village of Cáñar in the mountains. Packing in 24 switchbacks, some no more than a few hundred metres apart, this climb takes you on a beautiful journey to the edge of the Sierra Nevada National Park. Although there are spikes of 15% gradient, they are few and far between, making this a comfortable ascent; however, with an average of 7%, it's no pushover. Just under three kilometres after leaving Órgiva and with five of the climb's tight bends behind you, take the left turn which leads you on to the road to the summit. It's from here that the frequency of bends increases as the road zigzags across the empty hillside at an accelerating rate. With no trees to interrupt your line of sight, the views are consistent and ever-changing as you switch right to left to right with rapid frequency. Lined with high walls of chalky white rock or teetering on the edge of a vertical drop, this fantastic piece of civil engineering creeps ever higher. Upon reaching the summit in the centre of Cáñar, you can either reward yourself with refreshments or, if you're looking for a bit more altitude, take the road out the back of the village for some adventures on gravel roads.

FACTFILE

DIRECTIONS: On the western edge of Órgiva turn off the A-348 and head north on the A-4132 away from the roundabout.

SUMMIT ALTITUDE	1026m
HEIGHT GAIN	562m
MAXIMUM GRADIENT	15%
AVERAGE GRADIENT	7%

MAX GRADIENT **15%**

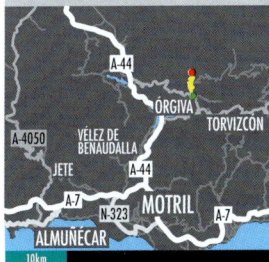

This one is a beast, with many stretches of double-digit gradient that pack a solid punch right from the get-go. The start lies in Torvizcón and is blunt to say the least as you pass the rather alarming 'ATENCION TRAZADO PELIGROSO' sign adorned with not one but three red warning triangles AND a 30kph max speed request. 'EXTREME PRECAUCION' is also recommended, so maybe click down an extra gear as you head into the wickedly steep hairpins that winch you out of town. On a narrow road squeezing through the almond groves, you ride in a giant arc up to the next set of nasty bends where once again you'll need to put in some serious effort as the corners spike close to 20%. Soon after, the climb begins to track due south, seemingly in a direct line up the side of the mountain, while behind you the most fantastic views unfold across the Sierra Nevada. This punishing stretch lasts for over 500 metres and is maybe the hardest bit of road I have cycled in the region. Once over the top it levels for a while before climbing again, this time not as harsh but still with the same epic panorama. After a second small descent, the finish arrives at a T-junction where you can take a breather or continue upwards on one of the many routes that lead to Haza del Lino.

FACTFILE

DIRECTIONS: Head east from Torvizcón up the steep street away from the A-348, following the signs to Contraviesa.

SUMMIT ALTITUDE	1256m
HEIGHT GAIN	596m
MAXIMUM GRADIENT	20%
AVERAGE GRADIENT	5.8%

MAX GRADIENT **20%**

10.2km

78 La Carretera de la Cabra

La Carretera de la Cabra (The Goat's Path), as it's known, was once the favoured route from the coast used by traders to transport their produce to Granada. A classic Andalucían climb that runs for a massive 35 kilometres, it takes you from Almuñécar on the edge of the Mediterranean, right into the heart of the mountains. Boasting utterly spectacular scenery towards the summit, not to mention the views out across the water, this is a 'must ride' if you visit this part of Spain. Heading north and passing through the villages of Jete and Otívar, the real climbing doesn't kick in until the 14-kilometre mark where the early 2–3% slopes transform into 6–7% slopes all the way to the Mirador de la Cabra (Viewpoint of the Goat). It's around here that the rock formations which characterise the later stages of the climb begin, their towering, jagged columns creating a stunning backdrop to your upwards progress. Once past the viewpoint, there are a couple of kilometres with little or no altitude gain, and then it's time for the push to the summit through an almost peerless geological wonderland. Twisting between the exposed rock that glistens in the sun's rays, you squeeze through a tiny tunnel to arrive at the top of an utterly remarkable road.

FACTFILE

DIRECTIONS: From the roundabout just north of the tunnel under the N-340, head out of Almuñécar on the A-4050.

SUMMIT ALTITUDE	1339m
HEIGHT GAIN	1324m
MAXIMUM GRADIENT	10%
AVERAGE GRADIENT	3.8%

MAX GRADIENT 10%

34.6km

79 Haza del Lino

This is the perfect climb to ride in the cool morning air before spending a day splashing around in the clear waters of the Costa Tropical with the kids, NOT as I did at the end of the afternoon in stifling heat – I felt like a rotisserie chicken being slowly grilled by the fierce Andalucían sun. I chose this ascent to Haza del Lino simply because it had a convenient starting point, but there are at least five other ways to climb to the tiny village and its life-saving bar. Heading directly north, this route leaves La Guapa via a series of tight bends on an initially wicked slope, before easing back as it curves around headlands rising away from the sea. With ever-improving views across the azure waters, you ride through the parched landscape via multiple hairpins and the odd nasty spike in gradient to reach the village of Polopos. In front of a small café, the road doubles back on itself then heads for the junction with the A-4131 where you turn left. With all the hard climbing now behind you, these last few kilometres are a breeze as you track westwards to reach the summit where you will likely bump into other riders who have made a similar pilgrimage to find a cold drink at the popular watering hole.

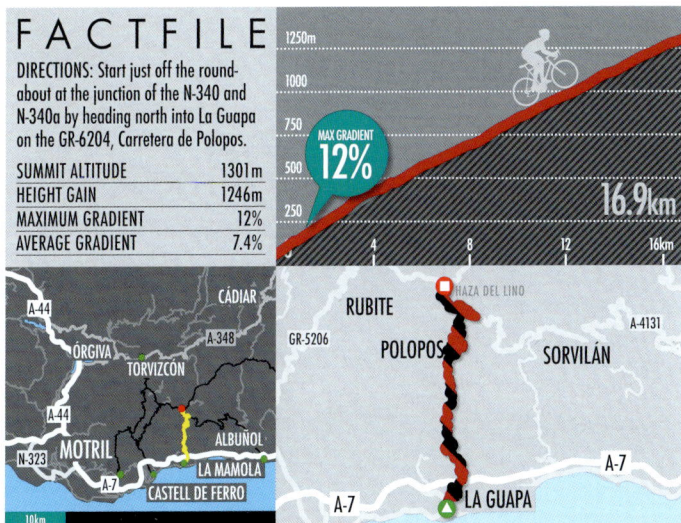

FACTFILE

DIRECTIONS: Start just off the round-about at the junction of the N-340 and N-340a by heading north into La Guapa on the GR-6204, Carretera de Polopos.

SUMMIT ALTITUDE	1301m
HEIGHT GAIN	1246m
MAXIMUM GRADIENT	12%
AVERAGE GRADIENT	7.4%

MAX GRADIENT **12%**

16.9km

Sorry for going on about the quality of Spanish roads, but this one, this one was off the charts; box fresh, it had yet to be opened to vehicles after receiving a sparkling new layer of tarmac. As cyclists are immune to 'road closed' signs, naturally I ignored the barricades that were set across the carriageway and pressed on so I could wallow on the dream-like surface, the whole road all to myself. I've chosen the southern flank of the climb from Cherín, a 25-kilometre journey to the midpoint of a road which cuts right across the eastern edge of the Sierra Nevada. The start is gentle, but after about three kilometres, through the village of Picena and up to Laroles, the slope becomes increasingly tough. With four out of the next six kilometres all averaging above 8%, be careful not to burn too many matches here as there's still a LONG way to go. After Laroles it calms down as you head through six hairpins set between the almond groves, then once these bends are negotiated your course is pretty much straight the rest of the way. Passing the turn to Bayárcal, you enter the national park to curve gently across the partially forested hills, then there's one last hairpin to reach the 2,000-metre summit where the slope fades in the shade of the surrounding conifers.

FACTFILE

DIRECTIONS: Start the climb from the large roundabout just south of Cherín, following the sign north to the Puerto de la Ragua on the A-337.

SUMMIT ALTITUDE	2041m
HEIGHT GAIN	1508m
MAXIMUM GRADIENT	9%
AVERAGE GRADIENT	6.1%

MAX GRADIENT **9%**

24.8km

81 Pico Veleta

Why do billionaires spend all that money building rockets to reach 'nearly space' when all they actually need to do is get on their bikes? The previous high point I had cycled to was the Cime de la Bonette, at 2,860 metres. The Pico Veleta stands 515 metres above that, and it is quite frankly OUT OF THIS WORLD. There are many combinations of roads to begin the ascent; I chose to ride from Pinos Genil up to join the A-395, used this for a while, then turned on to the A-4025, the quieter (and steeper) back road. After this, I rejoined the wider carriageway up to Alto Hoya de la Mora, where at 2,500 metres the air is already thin; it's here you begin the extraordinary adventure to the summit. Traversing the desolate landscape, you climb through endless switchbacks high above the world below, and as you do the road begins to falter. Before long, cracks start to appear in the once-smooth tarmac, these cracks turn to holes, then patches of broken surface, then with a couple of kilometres to go it turns to horrendous gravel. On 25-millimetre tyres, it became all but impossible to ride, and with 500 metres to go I had to throw in the towel. Once I'd stopped, I looked out across the curvature of the Earth, then down at the two wheels that had carried me to this point, and just shook my head in disbelief.

FACTFILE

DIRECTIONS: From the centre of Pinos Genil start your clock once you cross the Río Genil, then head east on the A-4026 and keep right at the first roundabout.

SUMMIT ALTITUDE	3375m
HEIGHT GAIN	2608m
MAXIMUM GRADIENT	14%
AVERAGE GRADIENT	6.5%

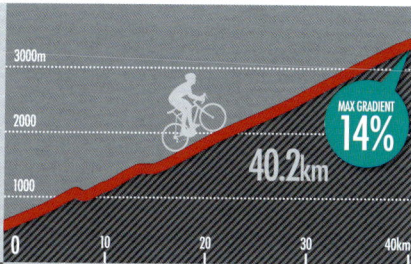

MAX GRADIENT 14%

40.2km

GRANADA

PINOS GENIL

MONACHIL

OTURA

PICO VELETA

PINOS GENIL   GÜÉJAR SIERRA

MONACHIL

ALTO HOYA DE LA MORA

PICO VELETA

As dawn broke, it was already approaching 30 degrees as I clipped in to begin my ascent of a legendary road they call the 'Alpe d'Huez of the desert'. Could it – would it – be as amazing as I had read and heard? Rising out of the Tabernas Desert, the vast arid landscape that famously doubled as the Wild West in Sergio Leone's Spaghetti Westerns, I had butterflies in my stomach. The first six kilometres into Velefique are set in a straight line, then, just before you reach town, there's a large, faded sign that gives you an outline of what lies ahead: 13 kilometres of 8% average gradient that rises no steeper than 11%. What this sign can't tell you is just how special those 13 kilometres are, or how you will be VERY unlucky if you cross paths with even a single car, or of how pristine the road surface is and how you will pass through a total of 22 hairpins (one more than Alpe d'Huez) on your way to the high-altitude summit. The sharp bends are sporadic at first, but six kilometres from the top you hit the golden section where their frequency will send you dizzy. High above the desert and set in truly extraordinary scenery, the barrage of twists delivers you to the summit of what could genuinely lay claim to be the eighth wonder of the world. WOW.

FACTFILE

DIRECTIONS: Heading north on the AL-3102 from Tabernas start just after the junction with the AL-4406 at the 'Término Municipal de Velefique' sign.

SUMMIT ALTITUDE	1825m
HEIGHT GAIN	1132m
MAXIMUM GRADIENT	12%
AVERAGE GRADIENT	6.2%

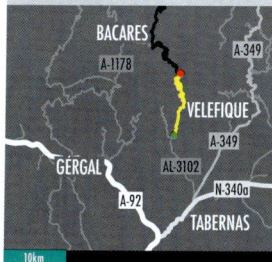

MAX GRADIENT
12%

18.2km

83 Calar Alto

If there are going to be folks looking for E.T. at the top, then you know you're in for a big ride. Just be thankful it's not your daily commute, because the summit of Calar Alto sits at a whopping 2,146 metres. Big brother to the neighbouring Puerto de Velefique, this ascent may not boast the same frequency of hairpins as its cousin, but it is nonetheless magnificent. A long climb at over 22.5 kilometres, it starts with a testing stretch out of Gérgal before hitting a small descent then taking the left-hand turn signposted to Bacares and Serón. With a modicum of tree cover, the climb offers chance if needed to shelter from the sun as you rise out of the arid desert into the slightly cooler air of the mountains. Deathly quiet, the road snakes through the patchy forest, steadily gaining altitude with the odd spike in gradient here and there to force a gear change, but nothing too savage. After 19 kilometres you reach a turn and following the sign to Calar Alto you do now hit a seriously tough ramp. Coming at the business end of this long climb, it will hurt the legs as you search for the twin white domes of the giant telescopes at the summit. Levelling out then dropping down, the final push twists through a small patch of trees to finish in the shadow of the observatories. Next stop, the stars.

FACTFILE

DIRECTIONS: Start from the roundabout just south of Gérgal and head north-east on Calle Pilanos, the A-1178.

SUMMIT ALTITUDE	2146m
HEIGHT GAIN	1416m
MAXIMUM GRADIENT	12%
AVERAGE GRADIENT	6.3%

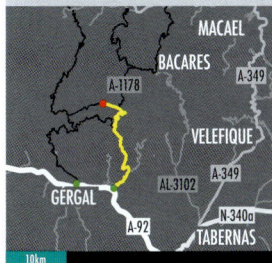

MAX GRADIENT
12%

22.5km

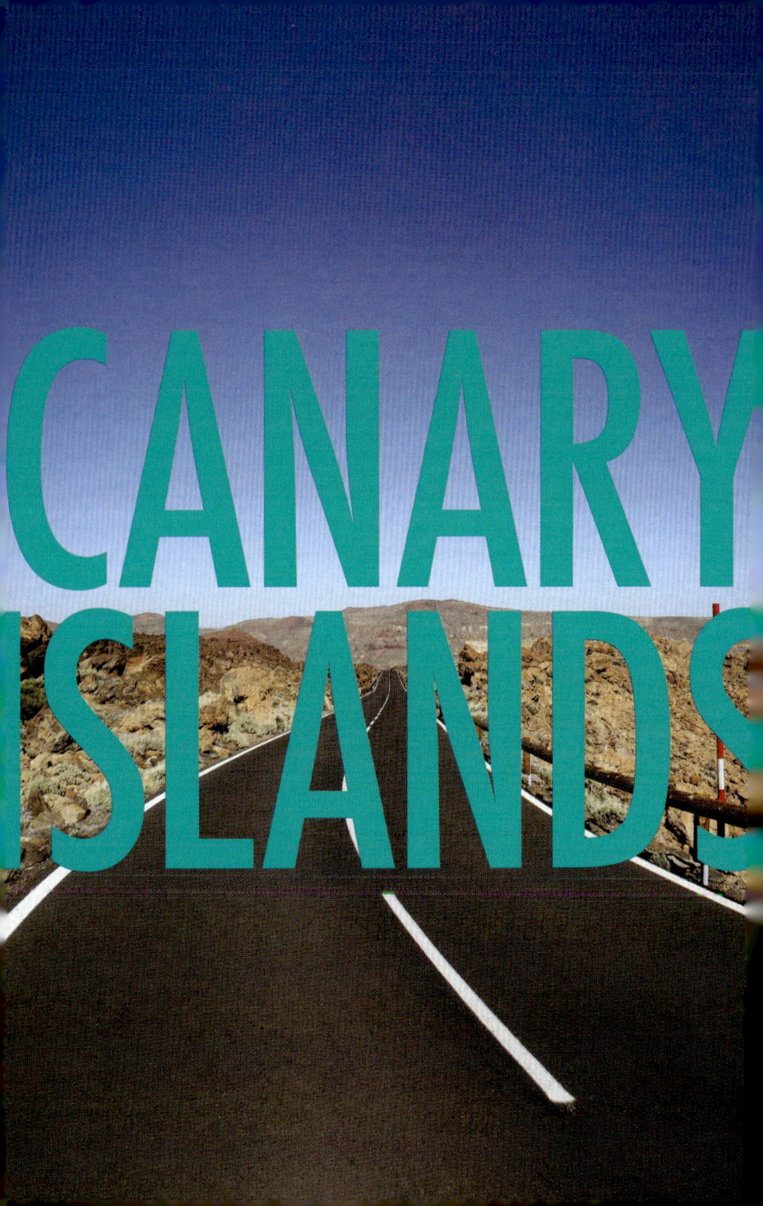
CANARY
ISLANDS

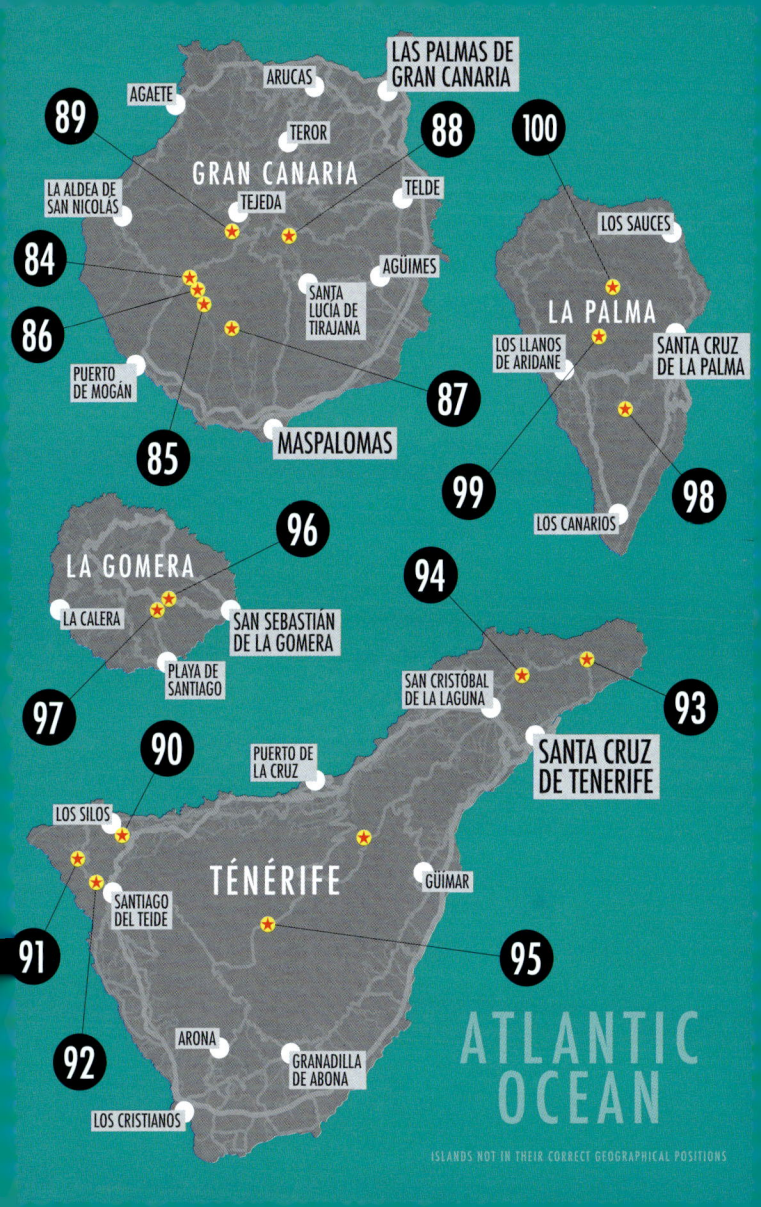

GRAN CANARIA

LAS PALMAS DE GRAN CANARIA

AGAETE

ARUCAS

TEROR

89

88

100

LA ALDEA DE SAN NICOLAS

TEJEDA

TELDE

84

AGÜIMES

86

SANTA LUCIA DE TIRAJANA

PUERTO DE MOGÁN

85

87

MASPALOMAS

LA PALMA

LOS SAUCES

LOS LLANOS DE ARIDANE

SANTA CRUZ DE LA PALMA

99

98

LOS CANARIOS

LA GOMERA

96

LA CALERA

SAN SEBASTIÁN DE LA GOMERA

PLAYA DE SANTIAGO

97

94

SAN CRISTÓBAL DE LA LAGUNA

93

SANTA CRUZ DE TENERIFE

90

PUERTO DE LA CRUZ

LOS SILOS

TÉNÉRIFE

GÜIMAR

SANTIAGO DEL TEIDE

91

95

92

ARONA

GRANADILLA DE ABONA

LOS CRISTIANOS

ATLANTIC OCEAN

ISLANDS NOT IN THEIR CORRECT GEOGRAPHICAL POSITIONS

84 Serenity

The moment I arrived at the end of this climb I immediately wanted to ride it again. I couldn't that day as I was out of time, but once back at the hotel I hastily rearranged the itinerary, scrapped my rest day and within 24 hours was back on its glorious slopes. Yes, it is THAT GOOD: it is quite simply climbing utopia. Some sources measure the climb's length from Puerto de Mogán and include the further kilometre on the tiny road that completes the Tauro Pass, but it's just the middle part I'm here for, the part they call Serenity. It's this section that this road is famous for, between the turn-off from the GC-200 and the T-junction 8.56 amazing kilometres later. Set on an immaculate surface, never too steep, and so quiet it feels like you could be the only human on Earth, it is packed with curves, hairpins, and twists and turns of every variety, and all set on a mild 6.6% average so you can potter up with ease or go at it full gas. Via 16 cactus-lined hairpins through towering red mountainsides that open up mind-blowing views, you are taken on a journey you will never forget. If you only have the chance to ride one road on Gran Canaria, make sure it's this one.

FACTFILE

DIRECTIONS: Serenity starts where the GC-605 heads north-east away from the GC-200, signposted Tejeda and San Bartolomé.

SUMMIT ALTITUDE	900m
HEIGHT GAIN	565m
MAXIMUM GRADIENT	12%
AVERAGE GRADIENT	6.6%

MAX GRADIENT **12%** 8.56km

85 Soria Pass

A climb of two halves – well, more like a climb of two thirds and one third – Soria is rightly one of Gran Canaria's famed ascents, and a must-ride for any visiting cyclist. Heading north from the southern coast, the road takes you deep into the interior to the secluded village of Soria which is perfect for a café stop before you explore further. To start, head north from El Pajar on the GC-505 under the motorway and trace the path of the river for about 14 kilometres on an almost unnoticeable 1–2% incline. Is this part of the climb? Can it really be included? I say yes, but you will need to be in the big chainring if you want to make it hurt. The transition to the 'real' climbing arrives as you enter the village of La Filipina and from here on it is most definitely not big-ring territory. Rising rapidly from the valley floor, the hairpins, cut from the red earth around them, squirm upwards, no longer on a 1–2% slope but now on something between 7 and 8%. Twisting skywards, they reveal views over the jagged canyons below, while the air is filled with the cry of peacocks (yes, that's what the noise is!). After five exquisite kilometres of climbing nirvana, the summit arrives as you reach Barranquillo de Andrés; it's straight on here for Soria, or, if you want a tougher test, turn left for three and a half brutal kilometres of very rough hairpins to the top of the Tauro Pass.

FACTFILE

DIRECTIONS: Start the climb from the roundabout at the base of the GC-505 on the edge of El Pajar and head north.

SUMMIT ALTITUDE	660m
HEIGHT GAIN	642m
MAXIMUM GRADIENT	10%
AVERAGE GRADIENT	3.3%

MAX GRADIENT **10%**

19.5km

86 Tauro Pass

At first, I wrongly assumed these crazy hairpins were part of the Soria Pass, but upon closer inspection they are indeed their own entity and thus can be categorised as such. You must complete the Soria climb first, then a handful of metres after crossing the summit in Barranquillo de Andrés, you catch sight of the start rapidly ramping up to your left. The contrast to the previous climb could not be more pronounced: gone is the smooth surface, gone are the sweeping corners and mild gradient; yes, this climb is a whole different kettle of fish. The total average may only be 7.5%, but taking into account the shallow final kilometre, the rest of it is pretty ferocious. Immediately ramping up to 15%, you climb past a scattering of houses in a straight line for a while, and then the corners arrive. First left, then a group of three hairpins, then a break, and then the signature bends: six switchbacks crammed into just 500 metres with each apex approaching 20%. The road cuts back and forth with increasing frequency, seemingly stacked upon itself, and – its broken surface strewn with rocks and stones – fights its way out of the valley. Exiting this tangle, the worst of the gradient is behind you; there are a couple more hairpins and then the slope ebbs away as you cross the exposed coarse landscape in search of the summit of this mad little climb.

FACTFILE

DIRECTIONS: The base can be found on the GC-505 in El Barranquillo de Andrés; take the turn heading west signposted to San Bartolomé.

SUMMIT ALTITUDE	926m
HEIGHT GAIN	269m
MAXIMUM GRADIENT	20%
AVERAGE GRADIENT	7.5%

MAX GRADIENT 20%

3.6km

GC-200 GC-605
SORIA
MOGÁN
GC-200 GC-505
PUERTO DE MOGÁN GC-1
GC-604
10km

GC-605
SORIA
GC-605
PIE DE LA CUESTA
GC-505
GC-200
EL BARRANQUILLO DE ANDRÉS

87 El Salobre

Of all the big climbs that head into the centre of the island from the towns on the south coast, this one is ridden the least (according to a popular ride-sharing website). Starting as you leave El Tablero and following the signs to El Salobre there's no hiding the fact that the early kilometres are somewhat scruffy. There is a bit of a litter problem around Gran Canaria's towns, and a penchant for fly-tipping. Thankfully, however, the higher you ride, the cleaner the roadsides become. Set on a super-smooth surface, with a multitude of steep ramps dotted along its undulating course, this climb offers a different challenge to the steady 7–8% incline you'll find on many other island climbs. Crossing desolate scenery devoid of any vegetation higher than a cactus, there are points where you'll see the road spread out for miles ahead as it picks its way upwards. Over small peaks, down rapid descents and through plenty of twists and turns, the increase in solitude and beauty as you climb is sensational. Following a final small descent and now deep in the canyons of the island's interior, the last ramp to the summit, punctuated with regular buildings, is seriously tough. A gruelling finale with spectacular views to complete an amazing road that carries you into the middle of nowhere.

FACTFILE

DIRECTIONS: Start the climb in El Tablero and leave the village following the sign towards El Salobre.

SUMMIT ALTITUDE	828m
HEIGHT GAIN	702m
MAXIMUM GRADIENT	16%
AVERAGE GRADIENT	4.8%

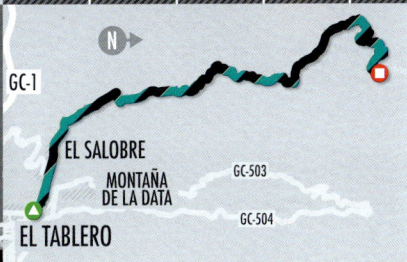

14.6km

MAX GRADIENT
16%

88 Pico de las Nieves

Pico de las Nieves sits at the very apex of Gran Canaria and there are endless permutations for its ascent, but I have chosen the route from Maspalomas up the GC-60 via San Bertolomé de Tirajana and Ayacata. Starting as you pass over the GC-1, the climbing is far from continuous with a few descents thrown in, but on the whole you head upwards for just shy of 45 kilometres. The first obstacle arrives as you reach the Degollada de las Yeguas viewpoint after six glorious kilometres of steady 6% slope. Followed by a short drop, it's then time to get stuck into the next stretch to San Bartolomé: 10 kilometres of super-smooth 6% gradient, through grand hairpins that boast expansive views down the giant valley. Heading west on the GC-60 and following a second brief loss of altitude, section three of the climb takes you to Ayacata which makes for an excellent pit stop. Up next is the hardest part – three kilometres of tough 9% climbing before the road begins undulating through the forested summit. This beautiful, tranquil environment is in extreme contrast to the deserted lower slopes, as you make two more turns – right on to the GC-130, then right again following the Pozo Las Nieves signs – on to the final 1,500 metres to the summit.

FACTFILE

DIRECTIONS: Head north out of Maspalomas on the GC-60 and start your clock as you leave the roundabout after passing over the Autopista del Sur.

SUMMIT ALTITUDE	1934m
HEIGHT GAIN	1844m
MAXIMUM GRADIENT	15%
AVERAGE GRADIENT	4.1%

MAX GRADIENT
15%

45.1km

89 Valley of the Tears

In the Valley of the Tears, as it's been affectionately named, no one can hear you scream. The VOTT is Gran Canaria's most feared climb, and for good reason: it is HORRIFIC. If you approach from San Nicolás, just reaching this amazing road is an ordeal as you venture through some real bandit country: rugged, frighteningly quiet and with more than its fair share of harsh gradient, especially up the switchbacks to the Presa del Parralillo dam. When you reach the turn on to the GC-606, this is where the VOTT starts proper. Ramping up through a swirl of 15% hairpins, this tough opening sets the tone for what's to come, and it gets a whole lot worse … Grinding through the savage, primordial landscape, on what is at times a dreadfully surfaced road, fear begins to creep in – fear of what lies around the next corner. You will soon be already in your lowest gear in anticipation, because nine times out of ten when you round a bend you will hit yet another 20% ramp. There are moments of respite through the villages of El Carrizal and El Toscón, but for the most part this road is industrial suffering on a surface that at times is almost rubble. The VOTT is simply relentless toil through a harsh, jagged and isolated wilderness. You've just got to love it!

FACTFILE

DIRECTIONS: Start the climb from the GC-210 that runs between La Aldea de San Nicolás and Artenara by turning south on to the GC-606 towards El Carrizal.

SUMMIT ALTITUDE	1360m
HEIGHT GAIN	1013m
MAXIMUM GRADIENT	18%
AVERAGE GRADIENT	8.5%

MAX GRADIENT **18%**

11.9km

Not first on most people's lists of climbs to ride on Tenerife, or second, or third for that matter, but this is one of the hardest roads – if not THE hardest – on the island. Linking Los Silos on the coast with La Tierra del Trigo, this formidable ascent is not for the faint-hearted. It may not seem like a long way at only 2.9 kilometres, but with an average of almost 14%, it can feel like 100. Leaving the pan-flat coast at Los Silos, you are faced with a wall of sheer rock ahead as you begin to climb at first in a straight line towards the ridge. The early slopes aren't particularly pretty – in fact, on the whole, this isn't the most beautiful road – but you're here to suffer, not get holiday snaps. After 500 metres, the bends arrive and for the next two kilometres you are thrust relentlessly back and forth into and out of the tight hairpins. With sections of 20%, and even 25% through the corners, at least the views are nice out across the ocean as you toil away surrounded by a myriad of palms and shrubbery. Finishing off this bonkers road, the final 500 metres are thankfully easier as you pass through the village of Las Arenas and up to the summit at the junction with the TF-423 where you can and most likely will collapse.

FACTFILE

DIRECTIONS: Head east out of Los Silos on the TF-42, then at the last roundabout turn south on to Camino de la Ladera which will lead you to the base.

SUMMIT ALTITUDE	489m
HEIGHT GAIN	397m
MAXIMUM GRADIENT	25%
AVERAGE GRADIENT	13.8%

MAX GRADIENT **25%**

2.87km

91 Monte del Agua

If you're heading for a date with the Wall of Masca, then it's more than likely that this will be the route you'll take on your way; a steady 11 kilometres of 6% average slope to get you warmed up for the hours ahead. Far more than just a warm-up though, this climb is well worth a dedicated journey to the north-west of the island. Leaving the Plaza San Sebastián in Buenavista del Norte, its course runs pretty much direct north to south and can be split into three sections. First, five and a half kilometres of switchbacks predominantly through farmland into El Palmar. Second, the huge, sweeping passage through the valley and its various villages on a slightly easier gradient. Then, third, the final winding push up the edge of the hillside to the summit at the Mirador Altos de Baracán. The gradient never climbs beyond 10% the whole way, making it a comparative doddle to climb even though it's reasonably long. Having said that, you will feel the pull of gravity a little more towards the top, but your major problem will be keeping your eyes on the road and not on the view out over the ocean. The vista across the valley and over the waves is sublime, however it pales into insignificance compared to the scene that awaits over the summit. Just you wait – it will blow your mind.

FACTFILE

DIRECTIONS: Leave the Plaza San Sebastián in Buenavista del Norte and head south on the TF-436, the Carretera el Palmar, through La Cuesta.

SUMMIT ALTITUDE	788m
HEIGHT GAIN	661m
MAXIMUM GRADIENT	10%
AVERAGE GRADIENT	5.9%

MAX GRADIENT **10%**

750m
500
250
0

11.2km

0   2   4   6   8   10km

BUENAVISTA DEL NORTE — LOS SILOS — TF-42
TF-82
MASCA — TF-436
SANTIAGO DEL TEIDE — TF-38

BUENAVISTA DEL NORTE
LOS SILOS   TF-42
TF-423   CRUZ GRANDE
LA TIERRA DEL TRIGO
EL PALMAR
TF-82
TF-436   LAS PORTELAS   ERJOS

92 Wall of Masca

This was the last climb on the last day of my first research trip to the Canaries, and it not only killed my legs, it dug a grave and buried them. I'd heard the rumours about the Wall of Masca, but they had somewhat gone over my head thanks to my preoccupation with Teide, but make no mistake: this road IS a wall. Also, to say it's a popular spot is a slight understatement. The road, its views and the village of Masca are favoured by tourists and cyclists alike, so if you want to avoid congestion on what is in places a very narrow road, then time your ride accordingly. Four kilometres at over 10% is just half the story; yes, this is incredibly tough, but it's also incredibly beautiful with jaw-dropping views over the valley as from Masca this wall snakes across the verdant hillside like that other wall, the Great Wall of China. Lined with neat concrete bollards and littered with hairpins where the gradient can spike as high as 20%, the road inches up the rock face in search of an end. The first time you reach what you expect to be the top, though, I'm sorry, it isn't. The second time? Nope. By now, your will is likely broken, so, thankfully, after two false summits, it's third time lucky and finally you reach the end of one HELL of a road.

FACTFILE

DIRECTIONS: Start the ascent from the roundabout at the eastern edge of Masca and follow the TF-436 all the way to the top.

SUMMIT ALTITUDE	1045m
HEIGHT GAIN	420m
MAXIMUM GRADIENT	20%
AVERAGE GRADIENT	10.8%

MAX GRADIENT **20%**

3.9km

93 El Bailadero

The far north of Tenerife is home to the Parque Rural de Anaga, a lush green region which is in sharp contrast to the barren, Mars-like landscape of Teide. There are several climbs, of which this one is the most prominent, that reach up from the ocean either side of the peninsula to summit at the ridge in the middle. Leaving San Andrés pretty much at sea level, the first few kilometres follow the wide valley as it creeps upwards towards the horizon lined with small green peaks. Before long, your immersion in nature (aside from the road of course) is complete, and in all directions you are met with the sight of the lush, interlocking mountainsides. Although far from savage, the slope does have moments of increased severity, with sustained periods of 8%, however, on the whole, as the 6% average indicates, this isn't an especially tough climb. With six kilometres covered, the hairpins now arrive to spice things up a bit. Passing through the odd small village, the wide road picks its way between the hills, the views improving with every pedal revolution. With two kilometres to go, there's a split to take cars through a tunnel, but keep heading upwards on what has become a much narrower road to the end of the climb at the junction with the TF-123.

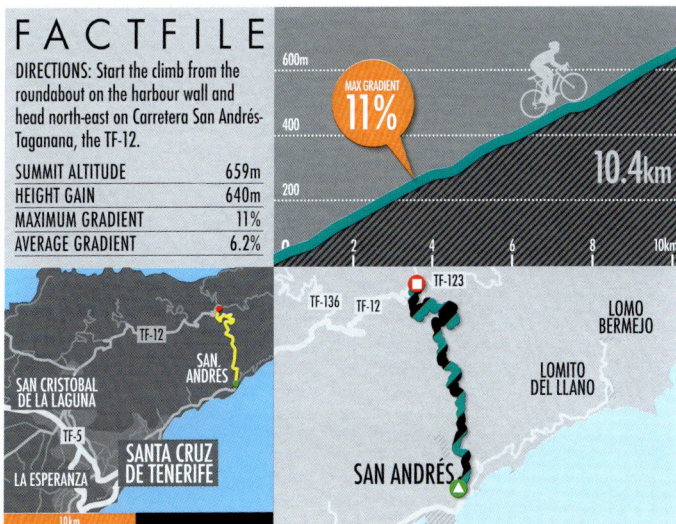

FACTFILE

DIRECTIONS: Start the climb from the roundabout on the harbour wall and head north-east on Carretera San Andrés-Taganana, the TF-12.

SUMMIT ALTITUDE	659m
HEIGHT GAIN	640m
MAXIMUM GRADIENT	11%
AVERAGE GRADIENT	6.2%

MAX GRADIENT
11%

10.4km

94 Pico del Inglés

Heading north into the Parque Rural de Anaga, this climb rides the ridge which divides the Anaga peninsula and delivers you to a place of heavenly beauty. You can trace the origins of the ascent to Santa Cruz de Tenerife, but to cut out all the urban congestion, I'm starting the clock where the TF-12, the Carretera al Monte de Las Mercedes, leaves the town of Las Mercedes and enters the national park. This does eliminate the first 12 kilometres of climbing, but it's the last bit you have really come for. With a 5.8% average, it's not too tough, but there are some nasty little ramps to contend with where the slope tips over into double-digit gradient – so be prepared. This isn't a climb to smash out in one big effort, it's one where you must stop to take in the views, starting with the sight of Teide from the Mirador de Jardina. After one of several short descents that destroy your climbing rhythm, you keep heading through the forest past the turn for the Mirador Cruz del Carmen (which requires a short detour) and then on to the final part of the climb. The ascent doesn't finish at the Pico del Inglés, but rather at the junction with the smaller road which then drops almost a kilometre to it, and once you have finished the climb you MUST carry on to this simply incredible vantage point.

FACTFILE

DIRECTIONS: Head north-east from Las Mercedes on the TF-12 from the roundabout at the junction with Carretera General a Punta Hidalgo (TF-13).

SUMMIT ALTITUDE	965m
HEIGHT GAIN	396m
MAXIMUM GRADIENT	12%
AVERAGE GRADIENT	5.8%

MAX GRADIENT
12%

6.8km

TF-143

TF-12

TF-13

SAN ANDRÉS

SAN CRISTÓBAL DE LA LAGUNA

TF-5

LA ESPERANZA

SANTA CRUZ DE TENERIFE

10km

TF-143

TF-143

PEDRO ALVAREZ

JARDINA

PICO DEL INGLÉS

TF-12

LAS MERCEDES

95 Teide

This is why you've come to Tenerife. All of the island's other climbs are just bit-part actors; Teide is the star, and rightly so. There are many ways to the top, and I urge you to ride them all, but I must choose one for the book and I have picked the route up from Los Cristianos via Vilaflor. The first part of the climb rises relentlessly past villages, a few welcome cafés and through the sparsely tree-covered mountainside. The views are magnificent, the road surface impeccable and the ascent pitched just perfectly on a 6.5% gradient. Reaching a peak after a mere 34 kilometres, you have essentially conquered the climb, but you have only just arrived at the best part. Crossing the summit, you roll across into an alien world of wonder that for all your life could be another planet. Crossing the vast plateau in the shadow of Teide, you soon begin to climb again to the famous Paradores Cañadas del Teide hotel. Here, pro riders check in to live at altitude to boost their bodies' red blood cell count so that when they return to sea level their blood can carry more oxygen to their muscles. However, this is of no concern to us mortals. We are just here for the sights and the journey up to the eventual high point of the road which is one of the most dramatic places you can ride a bike. JUST AMAZING.

FACTFILE

DIRECTIONS: Start the climb on the TF-28 once you have passed under the motorway (TF-1). Ride up to La Camella where you turn left on to the TF-51.

SUMMIT ALTITUDE	2324m
HEIGHT GAIN	2248m
MAXIMUM GRADIENT	10%
AVERAGE GRADIENT	4.6%

MAX GRADIENT 10%

48.9km

If it's an island paradise off the beaten track you're looking for, then look no further. Just a short ferry ride from the cocktails and nightclubs of Tenerife lies La Gomera, a volcanic cone measuring just 22 kilometres in diameter that is littered with fantastic climbs. The main settlement is the port of San Sebastián de la Gomera and this route is the best way to climb out to start a day's ride. Taking what is essentially the island's main road, you leave the harbour to begin a 22.9-kilometre upward journey to the centre of the Parque Nacional de Garajonay. It takes very little time to exit town then, via a huge switchback, you begin to climb through a long series of hairpins with almost uninterrupted views out to sea. Behind you, the colossal peak of Teide should be visible on the horizon as you romp up the beautifully wide, gently pitched slope as it next begins to track inland. The southern slopes of the island are sparse and barren, but once into the national park and the northern part that all changes. Suddenly, the dry, rock-strewn scenery is replaced by lush forest for the last couple of very steady kilometres which deliver you to the summit marked by a small roundabout.

FACTFILE

DIRECTIONS: Begin on Calle Cruz heading west from the roundabout next to the bridge over the river then carry on up the TF-713.

SUMMIT ALTITUDE	1354m
HEIGHT GAIN	1339m
MAXIMUM GRADIENT	12%
AVERAGE GRADIENT	5.8%

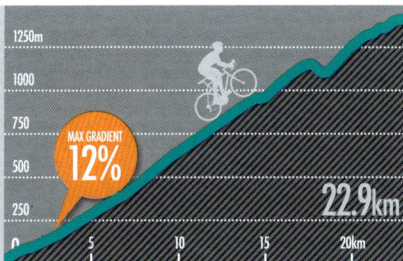

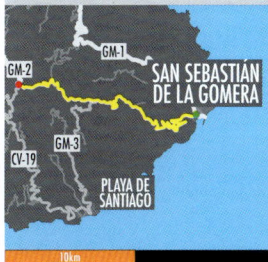

MAX GRADIENT 12%

22.9km

97 Montaña de los Ramones

I think it would only take a couple days to tick off every single road on La Gomera if you got to it, but unfortunately I only had one, so I just bagged three huge climbs, two of which made it into the book: the Alto de Garajonay, and this one. The climb that missed the cut was the lush, forested ascent from Playa de Santa Catalina; the shortest and easiest of the three, it also lacked the endless views out over the ocean, and so was left on the shelf. For the most part, the journey to the top of the Montaña de los Ramones simply traverses a bare hillside, switching back and forth with very little adornment. On a hot day like I had, it can be quite an inhospitable place to ride, giving the road a sort of nihilistic charm which I enjoyed. After 11 kilometres of relentless toil, the stark, barren slopes reach the village of Alajeró where you'll find a modicum of shelter beneath the odd palm before exiting back into the wilderness. Now, with a lack of hairpins, the road makes its way around escarpments of red rock and clumps of cacti and navigates around a large headland for one last uninterrupted view of the ocean before heading inland. The summit arrives at the boundary of the national park, where, as if by magic, the stark hillsides are suddenly covered with trees and bushes.

FACTFILE

DIRECTIONS: Leave Avenida Marítima on the harbour wall and head north out of Playa de Santiago on Calle del Santiago Apóstol.

SUMMIT ALTITUDE	1361m
HEIGHT GAIN	1351m
MAXIMUM GRADIENT	12%
AVERAGE GRADIENT	7%

MAX GRADIENT **12%**

19.4km

98 Alto del Pilar

From the little experience I gained while on La Palma, and backed up by plenty of photographic evidence on the internet, this climb seems to sit on the cloudy side of the island. I'm not a meteorologist so will not attempt to explain why, but my entire ascent was shrouded in fine mist, then, the moment I was over the top, I emerged into brilliant sunshine. Rising into the centre of the Parque Natural de Cumbre Vieja, the road up to El Pilar is a solid climb. With the sort of average gradient you'd find in the Pyrenees, this is a serious ascent, the first half of which zigzags up through farmland past the endless houses that litter the hillside. From bottom to top, the hairpins are set at pretty regular intervals, each one a carrot to aim for to aid your journey as you tick off the consistently tough kilometres through the mid-section of the climb. Not pretty to begin with but with nice views out to sea, the road's complexion improves the higher you rise: from scrubland to lush greenery, to towering pines as you cross into the national park. The gradient begins to ease over the last couple of kilometres as, in the shade of the giant conifers, you summit at the hub of outdoor activity that is the Refugio El Pilar.

FACTFILE

DIRECTIONS: To begin, leave the LP-202 just south of the village of Breña and turn west on to the LP-301 following the signs to San Isidro.

SUMMIT ALTITUDE	1488m
HEIGHT GAIN	1119m
MAXIMUM GRADIENT	15%
AVERAGE GRADIENT	8.3%

MAX GRADIENT
15%

13.5km

This is a magical road, deep in the heart of the island and leading to the popular viewpoint over the Caldera de Taburiente, one of the largest erosion craters in the world. At 10 kilometres wide, with walls that tower almost 2,000 metres high, it is beyond spectacular; hence its popularity, and hence this fantastic road built to reach it. Leaving the LP-3 just outside El Paso, head north past the visitor centre and then take the third right turn to start the climb. The slope is steady at first, then gradually begins to bite as it heads north through the tall pines. There are sharp spikes in gradient and small kinks in direction as you climb in the shadow of the towering mountain ridge to your right (where, if you're lucky, you'll see the amazing cloud formations pictured). Narrow, smooth, shaded and deathly quiet, the climb sticks to its almost arrow-straight course for 3.5 kilometres before the flourish of bends arrives. With a noticeable increase in gradient, the road makes its push for the summit and will now start to hurt the legs. As you snake through the forest, breaks in the trees offer monumental views down the valley which are guaranteed to stop you in your tracks before you reach the end of the road at the car park.

FACTFILE

DIRECTIONS: Head north from the LP-3 at the Caldera de Taburiente visitor centre on to the LP-302 following the sign to La Cumbrecita.

SUMMIT ALTITUDE	1312m
HEIGHT GAIN	471m
MAXIMUM GRADIENT	17%
AVERAGE GRADIENT	8.3%

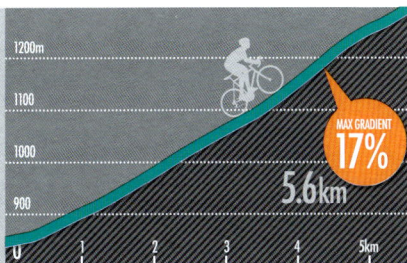

MAX GRADIENT **17%**

5.6km

1200m
1100
1000
900

MIRADOR DE LA CUMBRECITA

LP-202

EL BARRIAL

EL PASO

LP-3

EL PUEBLO
SANTA CRUZ DE LA PALMA
LA PUNTA
LOS LLANOS DE ARIDANE
LP-3
LP-3
SAN JOSÉ
LP-2
EL PUEBLO
10km

100 Roque de los Muchachos

This is the most mind-blowing climb I have ever ridden – and that includes the Pico Veleta. Forget Teide, that's just a lump, a mere blip. If you want altitude, if you really want an out-of-this-world island experience, then you NEED to ride the Roque de los Muchachos. Leaving Santa Cruz de la Palma there was moisture in the air as I began the giant ascent through the forest, but after 1,500 metres of vertical gain, the damp and grey were gone because I was now above the clouds. From here on, past the treeline, I entered a world beyond imagination above a sea of white that stretched far to the horizon. Crossing the harsh, sparsely vegetated volcanic landscape, with pure blue sky overhead and an ocean of fluffy cloud below, was simply unreal. At 35 kilometres in, you reach an intermediate summit at the Mirador de los Andenes, where, if you like, you can take a break to check out the Caldera de Taburiente before pressing on. Next, there is a three-kilometre descent before the astonishing finale. Home to a myriad of astronomical observatories, the mountaintop looks like the set of a 1980's Bond movie, and, taking the left turn, you wind up the final four kilometres between the huge galactic listening devices until you reach the car park at the top of the world. BEYOND EPIC.

FACTFILE

DIRECTIONS: Head north on the Avenida Blas Pérez González in Santa Cruz and start to climb as soon as the road goes up, first on the LP-1, then turn on to the LP-4.

SUMMIT ALTITUDE	2426m
HEIGHT GAIN	2422m
MAXIMUM GRADIENT	15%
AVERAGE GRADIENT	5.7%

MAX GRADIENT 15%

41.5km

¡Vamos!

To complete all the climbs in this book will take some serious commitment, however you will find many of them grouped in clusters which means you can grab a whole bunch on a single holiday, or 'training camp'. You then just need to work out how many trips ('training camps') you need to take to get the job done. Simple. For those of you not bothered about completing the list, you can just dip in and out and use it to add spice and drama to your adventures, taking you right to where the action is so you can ride the famous climbs you've seen on TV. Oh, and before you head off, especially if you intend to attack the real monsters, make sure you have the lowest gear at your disposal fitted to your machine – you will need it.

MALLORCA			
No	**Climb**	**Date ridden**	**Time**
1	Coll de sa Gramola		
2	Es Capdellà		
3	Coll des Vent		
4	Port de Valldemossa		
5	Coll de Sóller		
6	Coll d'Honor		
7	Col de Orient		
8	Alto de Puig Major		
9	Sa Calobra		
10	Coll de sa Batalla		
11	Puig de Santa Magdalena		
12	Coll de Femenia		
13	Talaia d'Albercutx		
14	Coll de sa Millera		
15	Puig de San Salvador		
16	Puig de Randa		

No	Climb	Date ridden	Time
	NORTHERN SPAIN		
17	Puerto del Portalet		
18	Collado de Piedra de San Martín		
19	Alto de Jaizkibel		
20	Puerto de Lizarraga		
21	Lagunas de Neila		
22	Arrate		
23	Puerto de Urkiola		
24	Monte Oiz		
25	Monte Sollube		
26	Picón Blanco		
27	Puerto de Orduña		
28	Puerto de Alisas		
29	Alto de los Machucos		
30	Portillo de la Sía		
31	Portillo de Lunada		
32	Peña Cabarga		
33	Fuente del Chivo		
34	Jito de Escarandi		
35	Lagos de Covadonga		
36	Collado de Llesba		
37	Alto de La Camperona		
38	Alto de l'Angliru		
39	Alto del Gamoniteiro		
40	Puerto de la Cubilla		
41	Cuitu Negru		
42	Ermita de Alba		
43	Alto de la Farrapona		
44	Puerto de Ancares		
45	Peña de la Escurpia		

CATALUÑA

No	Climb	Date ridden	Time
46	Mare de Déu dels Àngels		
47	Santa Pellaia		
48	Rocacorba		
49	Mare de Déu del Far		
50	Sant Martí Sacalm		
51	Santuari de la Mare de Déu del Mont		
52	Coll de Pal		
53	Coll de Pradell		
54	Coll de La Creueta		

VALENCIA

No	Climb	Date ridden	Time
55	Puerto de Almedíjar		
56	Puntal de l'Aljub		
57	Alt del Pi		
58	Coll de la Vall de Ebo		
59	Coll de Garga		
60	Coll de Rates		
61	Serra de Bèrnia		
62	Cumbre del Sol		
63	Puerto de Tudons		
64	Xorret del Catí		

SISTEMA CENTRAL

No	Climb	Date ridden	Time
65	Puerto de la Peña Negra		
66	Puerto de Navacerrada		
67	Puerto de los Cotos		
68	La Bola del Mundo		
69	Puerto de Navafría		
70	Puerto de la Puebla		
71	Puerto de la Morcuera		

No	Climb	Date ridden	Time
72	Puerto de Navalmoral		
73	Puerto de Mijares		

ANDALUCÍA			
No	Climb	Date ridden	Time
74	Sierra de la Pandera		
75	Fortaleza de la Mota		
76	Cáñar		
77	Puerto de Torvizcón		
78	La Carretera de la Cabra		
79	Haza del Lino		
80	Puerto de la Ragua		
81	Pico Veleta		
82	Puerto de Velefique		
83	Calar Alto		

CANARY ISLANDS			
No	Climb	Date ridden	Time
84	Serenity		
85	Soria Pass		
86	Tauro Pass		
87	El Salobre		
88	Pico de las Nieves		
89	Valley of the Tears		
90	La Tierra del Trigo		
91	Monte del Agua		
92	Wall of Masca		
93	El Bailadero		
94	Pico del Inglés		
95	Teide		
96	Alto de Garajonay		
97	Montaña de los Ramones		
98	Alto del Pilar		
99	Mirador de la Cumbrecita		
100	Roque de los Muchachos		

Muchas Gracias

'Thanks for driving us all the way across Spain and back, Dad. We didn't want to fly, honest.'

'Look, kids, you see nothing of a country if you fly, and anyway, as my role model Clark Griswold said, getting there is half the fun!'

Of course, none of these books would have been possible without the unwavering support of my wonderful family. They love mountains really, just where to take them next? Thanks to all my riding buddies who suffered the relentless pace of the family free research trips. Firstly, Owen Cooper in the summer of 2014, then Nick Burton, Ben Lowe, Paul Morgan and Chris Moores who accompanied me on various adventures to spectacular places. There was a bit of grumbling some days, but rest and relaxation is for when you get home, not for while you are somewhere exciting with new mountains to ride. Now get up, we leave in five minutes!

Thanks to the various resources that aided the production of the book, especially www.cyclefiesta.com, www.dangerousroads.org and www.cyclingcols.com Thanks to Cormac Keeney at www.sierranevada.cc for his advice on southern Spain, to Marcel Zamora for generously giving his time to show us around Cataluña and NO thanks to Covid for the two-year delay in production.

A MASSIVE thanks to Jon Barton and Vertebrate in Sheffield who saw the potential of the project when others did not; I hope we can work together on many more in the future. A big shout-out must also go to those who plot the route of the Vuelta a España each year and their commitment to the twin pillars of entertainment and suffering. Long may they continue to unearth insane roads to delight the fans, torture the riders and inspire us climb lovers to head off and ride them ourselves.

Finally, thanks to you for buying the book, and for your continued support of my little brand. I hope it brings you as much fun and adventure as I had making it. ¡VAMOS!

Coll de Sóller 497 m

ANGLIRU
ABIERTO

Puerto de Cotos

puerto de Alisas 674 m

Puerto e La Cubilla 1.683 m

Col du Pourtalet Altitude 1794

es Grau 468 m

Coll d'Orient 498 m

Altitud 2500 m

Jaizkibel 455

A GARROTXA

Picón Blanco

ROCACORB

Coll de ondreu 1010

puerto de Ancares 1669

puerto de Navacerrada 1880 m

Coll d'Honor 550 m

puerto de La Morcuera 1796 m

Puerto de eña negra 1909 m

PUERTO DE ALTO DE VELEFIQUE

Coll dels Reis 682 m

ort d'Eslida 620

Cura 534 m

Coll de sa Batalla 576 m

Haza del Lino

PORTILLO DE LA STA

Coll de Pradell 1736 m

Puerto de omiedo 1486 m

Puerto de Mijares 1.570 m

Pujada a SANT MARTÍ SACALM Sortida 815 m
Distància: 8,380 km
Desnivell: 604 m
Pendent mig: 7,2%

alto de La Cobertoria 1.173 m

ort/puerto de a Vall d'Ebo 540 m

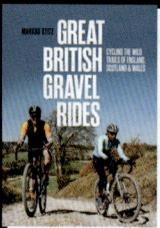

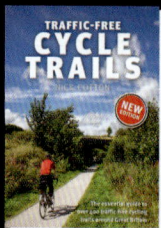